LOOKING BACK...........

THE STRUGGLE TO PRESERVE OUR ``` FREEDOMS.

BY

JOAN WILLIAMS

Our lives begin to end the day we become silent about things that matter.

- Martin Luther King Jr.

DEDICATION

This book is dedicated to all who have inspired me over the decades and contributed to my happiness, especially **Thor, Michele, Shadrach, Madelynn, Michelle** and **Bernard.**

ACKNOWLEDGEMENT

Special thanks to **Mark Smellie** who designed the cover, **Richard Foran** and **Geneive Cox** who carefully edited the publication. **Richard** also wrote the wonderful Foreword.

Another Yard Publication (September 2015) Revised

December 2016.

INTRODUCTION

I would never bore people with an autobiography as I have always found it quite tedious to flesh out the interesting parts of such publications, no matter how important and accomplished the subject is.

So while many people often lead us to believe that each of us who have lived as long as I have and have experienced so much *tumult, joys and challenges*, would have enough material to write three books, I have no such aspirations and will settle for this brief personal and political memoir.

Looking Back is therefore just a short rehash of some of the more interesting events that I was involved in, especially in the 1970's in Jamaica, when *political intrigue, the massacre of innocents and even treason* became aspects of our "democracy."

This was during the period when we fought an *undeclared* civil war.

The conflict was between communist surrogates, (nicknamed Soviets or socialists) and those of us who refused to surrender our freedoms and the democratic form of government to Russian imperialism. (Nicknamed CIA).

It was only the valor and resilience of courageous nationalists led a small group of opposition Jamaica Labour Party (JLP) Parliamentarians, some say with the assistance of the **American CIA**, which frustrated the communist takeover.

That alien ideology was being pushed by the Michael Manley government with the overt assistance of the **Cuban DGI** and the **Russian KGB.**

Having visited Cuba four times since then and seen how well the Cuban government succeeded in achieving the equal distribution of poverty and deprivation among the masses there, I make no bones about the fact that I am grateful to all, both external and internal forces, which stood up for freedom and democracy in our extraordinarily beautiful country, during that turbulent period.

I know there have been many publications written and circulated by perpetrators and propagandists from that era, geared towards sanitizing the horrible events that took place then, thereby distorting Jamaica's political history. But I feel I have a responsibility as someone who got more than a bit involved in the politics of the period, to present another side for those who were not around but wish to know the *truth*.

Interestingly, as I reflect on our own dark period, hearing the current disturbing news coming regularly out of oil- rich Venezuela concerning the similar devastating, oppressive and brutal effects of their socialist experiment some 40 years after ours, I wonder, do humans never learn?

Of course, all the conclusions I draw in this publication and the total dislike for communism/socialism which I have no qualms about expressing, are based on *my* experiences and observations from a position close to the action.

The most unfortunate thing though, is that after we defeated the socialist/communist threat, the politicians in Jamaica have through their close association with gunmen and the "bastardization" of the Westminster model, caused this, the fairest of islands, to have achieved and continue to retain a permanent position among the top *five* murder capitals of the world.

The corrupt mishandling of the economy by our leaders during the first half century of our independence, has also catapulted our country into becoming among the top *three* most indebted in the world.

Consequently, today deprivation still stalks the land, keeping over a fifth of our population living below the poverty line while the gap between the rich and the poor forever widens.

Despite these sad realities, the Jamaica the outside world knows is one with a very positive image. This is because of our country's natural beauty and profusion of unique attractions among which we can count our numerous talented musicians, the Rastafari culture and outstanding sportsmen and women who continue to *wow* the world with their record-breaking performances.

Thank God for these great Jamaicans as our political progress since independence in 1962 has really been dismal, brutal and sad and this is what I reflect on most.

There is also one chapter, "To Hell and Back," in which I reflect on my own very personal tragedy caused by the murder of my only son, over two decades ago. This is not to gain sympathy from readers though but rather to try and really come to terms with it myself for the first time. For even now, at times when the phone rings, I answer with trepidation as if I expect the same voice that told me of his death then, to be on the line. And who knows? Maybe by sharing my experiences in the deepest of pits and the hard road to recovery, I can assist someone who has had to walk this heart wrenching trail, feel less alone.

Apart from that, my life has been full of joy, success and laughter and I have also chosen to share some of the lighter experiences with readers to keep reminding myself of the pleasantries, so I too can continue laughing, for that is truly the best medicine. For if we cannot laugh at ourselves, do we not get swallowed by the myth of our own importance or allow ourselves to be weighed down by depressing thoughts?

I hope you will get at least one giggle out of some of the lighter experiences that I have chosen to share with you.

TABLE OF CONTENTS

PART 1

PART 2

FOREWORD

Oscar Wilde wrote, "Memory is the diary that we all carry about with us". Memory is the mental recording and filing away of experiences that can be drawn upon when the time is ripe and opportune.

And "the worst part of holding the memories is not the pain. It's the loneliness of it."

"Memories need to be shared", Lois Lowry wrote in The Giver.

In **Looking Back**, Joan Williams has delved into her memory diary and, in so doing, invites us to look into that memory bank with her and to face what is reflected back at us.

However, it is not easy to avoid the pitfalls of personal biases, prejudices, and boredom when one narrates, with the benefit of hindsight, one's personal thoughts and feelings of a life lived through the entangled political and economic realities of Jamaica during the turbulent decades of the seventies through the nineties.

Looking Back is a deeply personal, social and political commentary on those hard times for the Jamaica people. What Ms. Williams presents in her book are not the conjectures of a guilty or disinterested bystander but rather the passionate and humorous analysis of a deeply committed and active agent in the politics of Jamaica. Anyone who knows Ms. Williams personally or through her weekly Talk Show *Joan Williams on Line*, can verily testify to her passion and commitment to the upliftment and enhancement of all that is good about Jamaican life and culture.

She has been scarred along the way by personal tragedy when her only son was murdered and what transpired in the political arena over the past several decades has likewise damaged the Jamaican psyche. And, despite her scathing critical political analysis, she remains a hopeful prophetic presence for the future.

Indeed, her sense of national & personal independence expressed in the belief which she holds dear, namely, the inviolable nature of individual & personal freedoms allied to democratic forms of government is a major strand that holds together the different segments of this entertaining book. The mixture of social commentary, political analysis and personal family history offer an intoxicating mix for anyone interested in the recent post-independence history of Jamaica and the effects of international politics on Jamaica.

While it may be still too early for social and historical researchers to offer a substantial definitive version of those times, Ms. Williams' volume offers us a sense of the emotional immediacy of the period and how it impacted on individuals and the national psyche. For this alone she deserves our appreciation and heartfelt thanks.

One of the great advantages of this interesting volume is that readers of a certain generation will immediately relate to, if not always agree, with Ms. Williams observations and commentaries. Readers who have gone through those times with her, and who have been in a certain sense, *traumatized* by the same events will feel borne along as one of her companions on this road much travelled, and like her, have emerged with hope in the future.

Someone once observed that "the past is a foreign country; they do things differently there". Younger readers who cannot personally relate to those times will nonetheless perhaps recognize from their own contemporary experiences the impact of what Ms. Williams claims are the effects of those recent past events. And when we come to the end of this work, we might well ponder the words of William Faulkner, *"the past is never dead, it is not even past"*.

PART 1

POLITICS, DISGRACEFUL POLITICS

I have never particularly liked guns for the loud sound of gunshots annoy the hell out of me. But since the early 70's the harsh sound of gunshots and the bloodshed that it has left in its wake, have become a permanent feature of our lives in Jamaica.

Anyway, when I was growing up, I never saw anyone shooting a gun or even hearing the noise although my mother on occasion did leave evidence of having fired off a round or two.

My father loved to shoot birds and kept a double- barreled rifle. However, being the Collector of Taxes in Black River, the capital of the south western parish of St. Elizabeth, and living some 17 miles away from our home in Malvern, he only came home on Wednesdays and weekends as it was easier for him to stay with his mom in nearby Middlequarters. As she lived alone, he felt it was his duty to spend more time with her anyway.

For our protection therefore, he left his gun with my mom, showing her how to load it and shoot, I assume.

Apparently, that gun had a hell of a kick which my mom never learnt to control. So, on one occasion, I woke up in the morning to see a huge hole in the ceiling of our front verandah and was informed that she had heard suspicious sounds on the lawn, had loaded it and fired to scare off possible intruders. The problem was our lawn was several feet below the verandah, for as I recall we had to climb about a dozen steps to get up to the landing from the lawn. Somehow however she had managed to send a bullet some 20 to 30 feet into the air rather than downwards. Such was the kick.

On another occasion, I woke up to see a huge hole in the wall between her bed and the ceiling of the bedroom. She had again apparently heard strange noises and had gone to get the gun, which she laid on the bed. As she attempted to load it, it went off leaving evidence in the wall of why she should not be allowed to use that gun. I suspect my father eventually came to that conclusion and removed it from our house as I don't recall ever seeing it again or seeing any further evidence that she had used it.

I did manage to stay far from guns most of my life but since in Jamaica, politics, murderers, and guns have walked hand in hand ever since we got independence in 1962, I came face to face with this reality when I got involved in politics. In retrospect, even if I had not gotten involved with politics, as guns are now an integral part of our landscape, I would nevertheless have seen and heard about the effects on the society anyway.

When I became a political activist, I actually considered running for a parish council seat in the St. Catherine Parish council, with the ambition of possibly becoming Spanish Town's first female mayor. (St. Catherine, is the adjacent parish to the west of the combined parishes of Kingston and St. Andrew, in which the capital city Kingston is located.)

However, I now thank my lucky stars that I was quickly

turned off party politics before getting too seriously entrenched in organizing at the local level.

I need to give you some background about my earliest exposure to politics before we get there however.

I grew up in the countryside when the late Sir Alexander Bustamante was leader of the Jamaica Labour Party (JLP) and his cousin, Norman Manley, leader of the Peoples National Party (PNP), the other major party.

They were apparently quite outstanding people, Manley, a brilliant trial lawyer and Bustamante as a militant labor leader. Many persons spoke highly of them both, although some did try to ridicule Bustamante.

My parents, like most of the educated people in Jamaica at the time, boasted that they supported Manley as he was articulate and highly educated unlike his cousin Bustamante who some insisted (falsely) was illiterate.

Interestingly while it was accepted that the poor and downtrodden would support Bustamante, amazingly, so did the very rich property owners.

So contemptuous were the so-called educated elite of the "illiterates" who supported the JLP, that when they spoke among themselves, rich and poor JLP supporters were referred to as "Dutty Laborites" meaning they were poor, dirty, illiterate field-hands.

Incidentally, I had thought such a reference to our fellow Jamaicans had fallen by the wayside as we became more

16

civilized, but obviously not. For in 2014, a young PNP representative and junior minister, Damion Crawford, while speaking to his supporters, referred to JLP supporters using that same derogatory term. He clearly did not remember that the press was covering the meeting and had to quickly apologize when he was condemned by the public. But it is obvious that this is how many of the PNP "elite" still refer to the other side when the press is not around!

A Childish Prank

When I was growing up in Malvern, no one wore their politics on their shirt sleeves and I only heard mention of party or politics when an election was imminent. Still however, everyone seemed to know which families in the community supported which party.

I guess because I was young and it was my desire to oppose everything my parents stood for, why during one or two elections, I would climb a tree by the roadside and shout out to by-passers to VOTE JLP!

I never realized what an impact that childish prank had on some who took politics to heart until some 55 to 60 years later!

This I discovered quite by accident as I heard by the way that a lady who had been my "hero" when I was a child growing up, was 98 years old, still articulate and was living at a nursing home nearby.

Her name was Millicent Knight and she was the aunt of a prominent PNP senator K. D. Knight. Miss Knight was known to be a brilliant mathematician and a teacher at Bethlehem Teacher's College right there in Malvern, when I was a child. She later became headmistress of Westwood School, a prestigious girl's boarding school in the northern parish of St. Ann. After she retired from that position, she accepted the job of Deputy Headmistress at Hampton School, her, and my alma mater.

I recall Miss Knight with great admiration as she was the first black woman, I had ever seen driving a car. Further it was rumored that she had been the first black girl to attend Hampton Girls School and that story was even embellished to the extent that some people claimed she had to put white powder on her face to enter those hallowed gates, at a time when only rich white girls were admitted to that then racist institution.

What I really loved most about Miss Knight who was a close friend of my parents, was how she jigged and danced when she played the piano or pipe organ at church. This was the ultra-conservative Moravian church in Malvern, where the service was boring with no one moving to any of the music which backed up the hymns. I think they were taught that you would go to hell if you stirred in any way or even moved a muscle during a church service!

Anyway, my Miss Knight was the organists and while I recall her always dressing conservatively in white and wearing a broad hat as she walked demurely up the aisle from the back of the church to the front where the organ was, the minute she started playing, it was as if she was transformed into a "leggo beast." (Wild animal!) That is what I admired most about her,

18

the fact that she demonstrated that someone in *that* church had some life and moved vigorously to the music!

As she was a friend of my parent's, I had lost contact with her as she moved on and in fact had forgotten all about her until I heard she was in the nursing home nearby. So, remembering my great admiration for her, I called her there.

Naturally, as she was an adult when I was admiring her, she had no idea who I was. So, in an effort to jog her memory, I mentioned that I was the daughter of the late Collector Marshall, which is what my father had been fondly referred to by all, being the senior Collector of Taxes for the parish of St. Elizabeth.

She immediately replied, "Oh yes, he did have a rude little daughter who used to swing on the gate!"

Now that had to be me, she was referring to since my parents had only two children, my brother Bernard and I.

Nonetheless I was puzzled by that remark as I thought *all* children swung on gates. So, I could not imagine why the childish act of swinging on a gate was being referred to by her as being "rude."

Anyway, I decided to still visit her as I heard she had retained her fantastic memory, thus making her a walking encyclopedia who someone as curious as I, needed to tap into.

So off I went to try and benefit from her great knowledge and experiences, especially about life in the "olden days" in a deep rural community like Malvern.

As I saw her though, my curiosity got the better of me so the first question I asked was "Why did you say I was rude to swing on the gate when all kids swing on gates?

Dad. Joubert, mom Madeline, brother Bernie

Her reply really shocked me, for she said immediately "Your parents were staunch PNP supporters and you used to swing on the gate and shout to people to vote JLP".

You could have hit me down with a straw, for to begin with, I did not remember doing that from a gate but a tree. More importantly however, I could not believe that a childish prank could have had such an impact to the extent that an educated person like Miss. Knight would have let it bother her for almost 60 years!

For up to that point, in my mind *cultists* were only to be found among the unthinking and uneducated followers of our two dominant parties. And Miss Knight could never ever be classified as being unthinking or uneducated especially since she had been my "hero" when I was growing up!

Dangerous Garrison Politics

That is when it really got me thinking how lucky I had been to have been born in a peaceful rural community in Jamaica, rather than in what we call a "garrison." For in the garrisons, which are a contamination to the Westminster System of Democracy, political affiliation means everything to everyone and even today it is often considered a capital offence not to support the party that controls a garrison area.

So if a child who lives in a JLP or PNP garrison in Jamaica, playfully calls out to persons saying they should vote for the opposing party, either the parents, the child or all of them will quite likely have been harmed, their home burnt and the family chased from the area.

Although much has been written about the Jamaican garrisons, let me give an overview about this bloody phenomenon which was developed by our *power crazy, blood thirsty politicians.*

It has long been recognized that it is due to the nurturing of the garrisons, why since the 90"s Jamaica has been consistently recorded among the top five murder capitals in the world and rated as an extremely corrupt nation.

As successive governments have always chosen to quiet minority dissenting voices (recently sarcastically mocked and labeled as being the "articulate minority" by former PNP Minister Robert Pickersgill) and minimize overseas scrutiny by setting up committees or holding commissions of enquires into troubling topics then ignoring the recommendations, in 1997 a National Committee was established to look into

21

"political tribalism, garrisons and the violence they engender," under the chairmanship of a retired judge James S. Kerr O.J, QC.

Referring to Jamaica's unique "democracy" which includes numerous garrisons, the report which was laid in parliament in July 1997, stated in part that;

> *"Political garrisons were not a natural outgrowth of a political process but rather were nurtured and nourished as strategic initiatives to secure or retain political power."*

After the ceremonial tabling of the report was completed, the recommendations were totally ignored and the document sent to languish in the Library at the Institute of Jamaica while the garrisons and the powerful politicians who control them, have grown from strength to strength.

In fact so ingrained has the garrison phenomenon which is the root of our entrenched violence and murderous society become, that in 2016 Dr. Christopher Charles, senior lecturer in political psychology at the University of the West Indies, conducted a study into the pathological behavior by some young men in the dangerous garrisons and concluded in part that;

> *"Some 21 per cent of Jamaica's MPs (members of parliament) contribute to the murderous environment of garrison constituencies because they represent and benefit electorally from the undemocratic politics practiced in these communities. Therefore, these legislators provide tacit support for gang-based*

psychopaths in Jamaica. The country's high homicide rate has nothing to do with the enslavement of Africans during British colonialism."

It is very clear that the retention of these numerous garrisons which exist predominantly in Kingston, St. Andrew, St. Catherine and sections of St. James, remain a dirty stain on the character of the so-called statesmen who have led us since independence and most of those who succeeded them. But do the politicians care? A resounding *no*.

Let me backtrack a bit though. According to my late friend Wilmot "Motty" Perkins who was Jamaica's most courageous investigative journalist and someone who closely monitored the development of politics from the 40"s, the first garrison was developed in 1949 in the PNP stronghold of Matthews Lane in Kingston by a former government minister, the late Wills. O. Isaacs.

Motty said this was called "Group 69." It was made up of violent party activists bent on attacking and disrupting the meetings of the JLP which had been formed in 1943 by Bustamante, after he broke away from his cousin's party, the PNP.

Bustamante had led the JLP to victory over the previously established PNP in the 1944 general elections, taking home 22 of the 32 constituencies which existed at that time.

It wasn't until the 60's however, that an entire constituency was developed into a garrison. This was in West Kingston where Edward Seaga was the Member of Parliament. He in 1980 became prime minister of Jamaica.

It was there that the JLP, under the guise of providing proper housing solutions and community facilities for the poor and needy, perfected the garrison structure, calling it Tivoli Gardens.

To establish a garrison involved packing the entire area with party supporters. Those who had resided there for decades before and who were not "certified" as solid supporters, were forcefully evicted, their homes burnt, their property stolen and some persons were even killed. The enforcement or *political cleansing* was carried out by a well-armed gang under the iron rule of a bloodthirsty local leader known as a "Don. "

So effective did the garrison become in controlling the people in the constituency and terrorizing their opponents, that in the 70's a Housing Minister in the PNP government, Anthony Spaulding, used his ministry and the Tivoli template to fast track the establishment of several garrisons for his party. (It is said that Jamaica's first female Prime Minister, Portia Simpson Miller, *was* Spaulding's favorite protégé and her constituency was one of those established by him as a garrison.)

Spaulding's effectiveness can be measured by the fact that today over 25% of our constituencies are either total or partial garrisons and the PNP presently operates more than four times as many as the JLP!

Interestingly, the garrisons tend to be represented by the most senior politicians in both parties. And when I say senior, I do

24

not mean old but rather persons high up in the hierarchy of the parties. For having a garrison is cherished as a kind of *perk* of seniority among power hungry politicians for whom, *the end justifies the means.*

This is so because when an election is called, the senior people do not have to campaign in their constituencies as the dons are there to ensure that everyone goes out and vote for the "boss." This allows the senior officials who have high profiles, to freely travel island-wide and campaign for the lesser mortals or weaker candidates in their parties. At election time too, it had not been unknown for some of the garrison representatives to end up winning more than 100% of the votes registered!

Furthermore, these senior politicians do not have to do any form of representation to improve the lot of the residents in their constituencies, for the dons are there to ensure that nobody dares to complain about poor conditions in these areas.

It is therefore not unusual to find that most of the garrison constituencies without doubt, have the most inhuman conditions of all the constituencies in Jamaica. In fact, it was often pointed out that the most depressing living conditions are today found in the garrison "represented" by former Prime Minister Portia Simpson Miller, Jamaica's first female prime minister.

The dons play other roles for their political masters too, such as acting as storm troopers to break up demonstrations against the government when their party is in power. Alternately, when their party is in opposition, persons from the garrisons are herded up to swell the numbers when they demonstrate and when political meetings are being held.

While during the 70's the garrisons were mainly directly financed from the public purse via corruptly awarded government contracts, because the communist experiment of the 70's caused a financial disaster in Jamaica leading to our GDP being depleted by around 25%, the dons and their gangs were forced to find other means of financing the luxurious lifestyle to which they had become accustomed. Consequently, they adopted other criminal means in addition to the largesse from the public purse.

In the 80's they started to include extortion and international drug smuggling to their activities. First they started with our local home grown marijuana exports and as they set up lines and structures to get their products safely into North America, many evolved to become masters in the cocaine trade, establishing links with cohorts from Colombia.

By the end of the 80's Jamaican drug dons had become major players in the international drug trade. However, no matter where they resided, they remained extremely loyal to their parties at home and consistently spent millions of dollars buying and sending arms and ammunitions to their party-affiliated gangs in Jamaica.

These *Yardies* as the notorious Jamaican drug gangs came to be known, gained such a reputation for their violence and thirst for blood, mainly in the USA, that new law enforcement teams had to be formed there to target and combat them specifically.

Eventually they were brought under control in the USA, either by being killed, imprisoned, or deported back to Jamaica and their rise and demise have been the topic of many books.

Unfortunately for us, those who were deported to Jamaica returned with a high level of sophistication in criminal activity and vast international links which our law enforcers, or rather, those who have not been corrupted themselves, have been incapable of coping with even now.

When you combine the Yardies natural tendency towards violence with the political protection that the gangsters continue to enjoy from powerful people in the JLP and PNP, you understand why our poor country still continues to be among the top 5 murder capitals of the world, a categorization we initially achieved in the early 90's.

Statistics also show that the residents of the garrisons contribute to some 60% of the violent crimes being committed locally. In addition, according to the World Bank, the GDP in Jamaica would be significantly higher had it not been for the crippling effect of crime on the island.

Crime and violence continue to destroy the country with families being directly affected through loss of life and indeed *quality of life.*

A climate of fear pervades our society (witness the rise of security companies over last few decades) not to mention the widespread cost to the economy, including diminishing

economic growth. A UN report connects crime and development in the Caribbean when it states "the Issue of crime & violence has become one of the most pressing concerns for Jamaicans. It has had a negative impact on all spheres of society and has been cited as being a major factor contributing to the low levels of GDP growth Jamaica has experienced over the last 30 years."
(http://www.unodc.org/pdf/research/Cr_and_Vio_C ar_E.pdf)

Even where a politician does not operate a garrison constituency as was the case of the longest serving prime minister of Jamaica P.J. Patterson, the dons know their role in repressing dissent and powerful political leaders do little or nothing to separate their party from those essential "functionaries."

For example, during the 1999 gas demonstration which elicited island-wide support because the government had pushed the price of gas up by instituting a massive tax on petroleum products, residents of downtown Kingston did not join in. It is alleged that this was because Zeeks, the powerful don from Matthews Lane (where the first garrison was established in 1949), made sure that downtown residents *stayed off* the streets.

When a photographer from one of the newspapers photographed and published a picture of Prime Minister Patterson downtown shaking Zeeks" hand shortly after the demonstration, it immediately fueled speculation that he had travelled there specifically to thank him for keeping the area quiet.

Then there was the "Heather Robinson affair" which gave then Prime Minister Patterson a perfect opportunity to clean up the garrison politics he claimed he had nothing to do with. He however chose not to avail himself of this opportunity.

For it was during his term as supreme leader that Donovan Bennett aka Bulbie, one of Jamaica's most cold blooded, murderous and successful gang leaders, established the "Clansman Gang." This gang not only received (and continues to receive!) open political protection from powerful people in the ruling PNP but also government contracts.

Bulbie was killed in 2005, but by then he had been linked to some 80 murders, had personally amassed a huge fortune and had made his gang into a dominant killing machine. In fact, long before *ISIS* started to horrify the world by beheading people, the Clansman gang had been horrifying Jamaicans with this chilling method of execution. For how can we forget the brutal murder of Charmaine Cover-Rattray who along with her daughter were beheaded in Lauristan, St. Catherine, while both were apparently still alive! And many other individuals in the Spanish Town area have been similarly executed by members of that gang.

Today this gang is number *one* in the extortion racket, using violence to intimidate business people, especially persons in the transportation and retail sectors. Their dominance spans from the municipality of Portmore to most towns in the parishes of St. Catherine, Clarendon and even Manchester, forcing people to pay them large sums of money for protection or they lose their lives.

According to an estimate from the police published via news release in May 2015, this gang rakes in $1.5 million daily in Spanish Town alone!

While their operations are often quite overt and many of the gang members are well known, because they receive political protection and have no compunction about killing "informers," on the few occasions when any member of that gang is arrested, they cannot be successfully prosecuted.

And while the police have the powerful Anti-Gang Legislation to deal with gangsters, because Jamaica has a notoriously corrupt police force, members of this gang can be seen in the Spanish Town market and bus park, openly collecting their extortion funds from poor, struggling vendors and transport operators, right in front of police officers on duty.

Why? Because most of the police have been paid off or instructed to look the other way. The poor vendors and transport operators therefore have no recourse but to pay. A similar picture exists at the markets and bus depots in several other towns.

I know as a fact that when Bulbie was allegedly wanted by the police for murder, he was often seen openly sitting in front of his block-making establishment located on the Spanish Town bypass road in St. Catherine.

According to police records, he was wanted for the murder of Derrick Eckleston aka Puppy String who himself had a fledgling gang. Eckleston was killed in the PNP garrison of De La Vega City in St. Catherine, in 1995 after being attacked by three Clansman members. After shooting and wounding Eckleston, Bulbie is supposed to have stood over the dying man and pumped several shots into him. While the other shooters were convicted and sentenced in the courts based on eyewitness reports, Bulbie was never touched and continued to leave behind him a path splattered with blood.

In the beginning, he had been the PNP's powerful strongman in the Central St. Catherine constituency which at the time was held by the JLP's General Secretary Bruce Golding (who later became prime minister from 2007-2011). Clinton Davy aka Jingles, a man with a questionable reputation himself, was the PNP's candidate and Bulbie's mentor.

When Jingles was defeated, Bulbie apparently thought his political protection might wane, so he moved and tried to hitch his wagon to the successful PNP candidate for South Central St. Catherine, Heather Robinson.

To her credit, Robinson has been the only Jamaican politician who has openly tried to extricate Jamaican politics from "gangsterism" and murder.

She even attempted to solicit the assistance of other elected legislators in parliament, but was overtly snubbed by her fellow parliamentarians who had apparently become so dependent on corruption and strong arm tactics, that they could not imagine retaining the power they so craved, without the assistance of their party-affiliated, armed gangsters.

When Bulbie moved into Robinson's constituency, he went on a killing spree of fellow PNP supporters in order to

31

establish his dominance through raw fear. By then he was a killer out of control who had publicly declared that he planned to become "...the only Don in Spanish Town and in fact the whole St. Catherine." This was in the mid-90's.

By 1996, his activities were causing major panic among especially PNP supporters who had been his main targets in the constituency. This was particularly so in the stronghold of De La Vega city where word was, he had said he planned to kill Robinson herself as she was resisting his overtures to become the leader in the constituency.

This threat, in addition to the constant bloodshed was apparently what convinced the representative Robinson to go to parliament to make an impassioned and desperate plea for assistance from her other elected colleagues and the party leader. There she pleaded with her colleagues to join her to dismantle tribalism and bring garrison politics to an end.

In her famous speech in Gordon House she declared that she was neither prepared to; "...hug up criminals nor give birth to a Don for in that regard I am truly barren." She also hit out at the old style of politics saying; "Some of the old dogs in our Parliament need to be taught new approaches." (The entire speech is recorded in Hansard.)

Her impassioned plea was however met with a stony silence by her colleagues on both sides of the house and word is she was side-lined by her party, which was led by P.J. Patterson at the time and in which the powerful lady, Portia Simpson Miller, who became Jamaica's first female prime minister, was a senior player.

Robinson resigned from politics soon after while Bulbie went on to prosper financially from his illegal activities and from becoming a major recipient of government contracts. Although he was killed in 2005, his gang has continued to leave a bloody trail even turning on each other regularly, as they fight over the spoils. The fact is, in the first week of May 2015, as two factions of the gang fought for supremacy, they murdered 11 of their own cohorts in Spanish Town area in just one week, according to the police.

Of course, as their political protection remains intact, one rarely hears of any of the murderers in this gang being arrested or convicted, as I suppose they are considered too valuable to the powerful PNP.

Robinson's stance had opened up the perfect opportunity for Jamaican parliamentarians to act to stem the bloodshed and mayhem which had by then started to envelop the country, causing the number of murders to move from a low of 172 in 1972 to 888 in 1980 and 1682 in 2009.

However, because the powerful politicians in both major parties depend on garrison politics for the power and glory they relish, Jamaica since the late 90's entered and has almost constantly remained in the league of the top 5 murder capitals in the world.

By 2008, the "garrisonisation" of the country had reached the point where even a separate "independent state" was established within one constituency, with a President to boot.

This was in the West Kingston, where a JLP protected criminal, Christopher Coke aka Presi and Dudus, was so treasured that he had become untouchable for decades, up to the point of his extradition to the USA. He had also become super wealthy as he too benefitted greatly from government contracts in addition to his illegal activities.

Dudus, was the son of the notorious Lester Lloyd Coke aka Jim Brown, who had ruled that same political roost at Tivoli Gardens for decades, while the former prime minister Edward Seaga was the representative of that violent garrison.

During the 80's Jim Brown took his Machiavellian talents to the United States where as the leader of the notorious, cold blooded "Shower Posse," he was reputed to be a major cocaine smuggler and arms dealer who drove terror into the hearts of law enforcement officers and criminals alike.

When the heat in the US became too much for him, he returned to Jamaica but was arrested in 1992 as the Americans demanded his extradition. While he was in jail in Jamaica awaiting extradition, he was mysteriously burnt to death in his jail cell although no evidence of flammable material was ever found in there!

Like most murders in Jamaica, his remains unsolved.

Jamaicans have long speculated however that he was murdered on the orders of powerful political persons who were fearful that once in the US, he would spill the beans. For he clearly knew too much about the ties between Jamaican politicians and their violent criminal associates.

According to persons who claim to know Dudus, he had often sworn that he would never allow himself to be similarly used and killed by his political handlers in Western Kingston and consequently he would never allow himself to be held in a Jamaican jail.

I have been mulling over a statement made by a former commissioner of police Owen Ellington in April 2015, while giving verbal evidence at the Commission of Enquiry into the deaths of between 77-150 persons killed when the police and army stormed Tivoli Gardens in 2010 to try and apprehend Dudus in preparation for his extradition. Interestingly, although so many persons were killed and hundreds detained, Dudus seemed to have easily escaped the police dragnet. (Many claim this was with the assistance of some corrupt senior police who were on his payroll.)

According to Ellington, in order to minimize the bloodshed, he had foreseen, a pastor named Al Miller had gone to encourage Dudus to give himself up. On his return, Miller reported; "I saw the man and the man say to me that if it was the PNP in power they would know how to deal with it."

Wow. I have been wondering ever since, what that chilling statement really meant!

We all know that criminals in the underworld, regardless of their differing political allegiances, often share notes.

So exactly what was Dudus implying? Is it that the PNP habitually spirit away their gangsters out of "harm's way" when they were wanted for murder as they did with George Flash and Tony Brown? Or could it be that the party had found a corrupt individual in the US Justice Department (oh yes they exist!) who was prepared to let extradition warrants for the PNP's dons disappear?

Regarding the George Flash/Tony Brown affair, in an interview with ace, impartial crime fighter Keith Trinity Gardner, we were reminded of those events not too long ago. This was via an article published on June 10th, 2012 in the Jamaica Observer. He said;

> "*In August 1977, I held George Flash in Vineyard Town on suspicion of murdering (Edward) Ted O' Gilvie. He spent a week in jail, but his lawyer issued a writ of habeas corpus and I was told by authorities higher up that we had to let him go. About a week later, I learned that he and Tony Brown were wanted for the murder," Gardner said. "This was for the killing of Ted O'Gilvie, a top public servant, who was killed at his Havendale home on June 16, 1977. Flash and Brown fled Jamaica for Cuba where they remained for 22 years. When they returned to the island, they were arrested by Criminal Investigation Branch detectives on separate days after they turned themselves in, accompanied by Burke. However, faced with a lack of witnesses the judge had no choice but to free both men of the charge.*"

The Burke referred to above was up to November 2016, the powerful General Secretary of the PNP and a close confidant of the then Prime Minister Portia Simpson Miller!

I have no idea what Dudus meant, but he was clearly hurt as he felt the JLP had not done enough for him or rather, as much as the PNP would have done for their gangsters.

Whatever he meant by that chilling statement, it does not augur well for us as it indicates that the ties between the two powerful political parties and the vicious criminals will not be broken any time soon unless by some miracle, we get rid of both the JLP and PNP!

I dare say too that had the American government not wanted Dudus for gun running and drug smuggling, it is quite possible that he could even have become an "elected representative" and maybe *even prime minister* of Jamaica, had he had such ambitions!

For he had become extremely popular among the people in the constituency because he operated as a modern day "Robin Hood" paying school fees for children, feeding the hungry and assisting many others financially.

It was not surprising therefore that when news of his being wanted by the American government broke, hundreds of the residents of Western Kingston demonstrated in the streets, vowing to defend him to the death.

Dudus' rise and demise will I am sure soon become the topic of many books for as I pointed out earlier, a Commission of Enquiry was held into the death of some say, over 150 persons who were killed when the police/army stormed his stronghold in Western Kingston in search of him in 2010. It is even said that outside gunmen from all over Jamaica had also gathered there to help defend him. It is interesting to note however that while so many persons were killed when the security forces went to capture him, Coke easily escaped!

Interestingly, the autopsies indicate that some 35 of the victims of that alleged confrontation with the security forces were shot in their backs, indicating that they were not killed in combat but were possibly *individually* massacred by our own security forces. That would not be surprising though, as our police force has long gained international notoriety for their penchant for carrying out extra-juridical killings.
Anyway, Dudus was only extradited after the Bruce Golding led JLP government had used *every* possible ruse, including recruiting a powerful US law firm, Manatt, Phelps & Phillips and paying them US $50,000.00, to try and prevent the extradition of their most senior don.

Golding's government only capitulated when the US government cancelled the visas of some powerful party supporters and that led to public pressure being finally put on the JLP government, for in Jamaica a US visa is more precious than gold.

It was the events leading up to this extradition in 2010 which really rubbed salt into our wounds. For the action of that government demonstrated just how quickly our political leaders were willing to sacrifice the international reputation of our sovereign nation to save their political gangsters.

And while some politicians often loudly insist that the ties between them and the gangsters no longer exist, one notorious hoodlum was recently even elected to the Executive of a constituency of the PNP. This infamous character was Kenley

'Bebe' Stevens, once described by the police as being the King of *Lotto Scamming* in Jamaica. Lotto scamming, is the activity that the police blame for the extremely high murder rate in the Montego Bay area. Since June 2015, the police said the parish of St. James in western Jamaica has had the highest murder rate in the entire island.

Further, this lotto scamming racket has damaged Jamaica's name badly as major international media houses including the prestigious Wall Street Journal, USA Today, CNN, CBS etc. have published documentaries about this scheme.

How it works is that potential victims in the USA receive a telephone call informing them that they have won a lottery. The targeted victims are then told that they need to pay taxes or administrative fees before receiving the huge prize. Some vulnerable and naive people pay fees totaling thousands of dollars, but naturally, they never receive any prize. Losses of hundreds of thousands of dollars are common. Most of the victims are senior citizens and despite frequent warnings to their citizens from the US authorities, the scam has flourished. According to reports, after losing their life's savings, some elderly Americans have even been driven to suicide.

At first, the American government warned their elderly citizens to be wary of calls emanating from the Jamaican area code 876 but when that had no effect, they started to put pressure on the Jamaican government to enact legislation to deal with the scammers. Eventually, the government enacted the Law Reform (Fraudulent Transactions) (Special Provisions) Act 2013.

It is ironic however, that while the PNP government was assuring the naïve Americans that they were doing everything to stem lottery scamming, one of the major players was on the executive committee of one of one their constituencies! For Bebe, who was killed in June 2014, was at the time of his murder, vice-chairman of the West Central St James constituency which was headed by the then minister of state in the Ministry of Industry and Commerce, Sharon Ffolkes-Abrahams!

Unfortunately, despite all these scandalous revelations and regular evidence of gangsters walking hand in hand with senior politicians, I still see no evidence that the necessary public pressure will ever be brought on our legislators for them to clean up their act. So I assume we will forever practice garrison politics and murder will continue to be second nature to us, despite the horrible reality that some psychopaths in our midst are now targeting our even our children. According to the latest statistics published in April 2015, a whopping 30 children have been murdered in this little island with a population of 2.8 million. The most chilling to date being the execution-style murder of three young men all under 16 years old, on April 21st, 2015 at Moneymusk, a quiet rural village in the mid-island parish of Clarendon.

The reason why I predict that there will be no parting of ways any time soon between elected representatives and their violent criminal cohorts, is because the vast majority of politicians, regardless of where their particular power bases are, have *benefitted* from the activities of the gunmen from the garrisons who help them to gain/maintain power.

I remember a good friend of mine, a PNP candidate, who had his base way out west in peaceful Negril, telling me how he came home one day in the 70's and found four rough looking men at his home.

They told him they had been sent by the party to "deal wid labourites" (labourites is what JLP supporters are called) in his area. Deeply disturbed that gun violence could break out in his peaceful region, he told me he had assured them that all was under control and sent them back to Kingston. He was an *unusual* politician indeed.

On the other hand, another acquaintance of mine, a former JLP candidate from the eastern parish of Portland, told me that he would forever have it on his conscience how two young men from his area had been convicted for murder when he knew it was not them, but gunmen who had been sent from the well-armed super-garrison of Tivoli Gardens to assist him, who had killed a PNP activist in his constituency.

As the dons have become more powerful in their political garrisons, some now even blatantly organize human trafficking activities. For it is well known that many young girls, are forced to go to the "dons" and other of their gang members to be deflowered as soon as they reach puberty. According to a statement from the police in 2015, this is what has contributed to the unusually high number of missing children in Jamaica. (2796 reported missing between January 2011 and April 2015 in a little island with a population of only 2.8 million.)

For indeed, so scared are some parents and caregivers about the type of initiation that young girls are subjected to by dons and their cohorts, that they sneak their children off to the country to live with relatives around the time they know they will be sent for. They then report the girls to the police as "missing."

The police have Anti-gang legislation and other laws to bring these child abusers to justice, but while laws are easily enacted in Jamaica to cover every ill, often where big money is paid or political pressure put on, little or no enforcement ever takes place.

Anyway, some other parents have no problem sacrificing their young girls for the free light, free water and free houses that the dons are able to organize in the garrisons. For by using violence, they keep away landlords from entering their *own* properties, also utility workers and collectors, all apparently with the tacit and sometimes overt approval of their political representatives.

So powerful have the dons become that some even supply workers for businesses in the downtown
Kingston area where they also provide "security". These workers have absolutely no rights. They are *forced* to accept any wage the don determines, privileges such as lunch hour, sick leave and even bathroom breaks are not allowed and in fact their lot is that of slaves of yore. But I guess, in return for the free houses, free light, free water that residents of most garrisons enjoy, their personal freedoms must be sacrificed. Those who do not wish to live under the thumb of dons and

other enforcers, must run away from these oppressive enclaves.

Disgracefully, these slave-like working conditions are no secret as from time to time persons share their experiences with journalists, anonymously of course. So it is clear the leaders who sit in parliament and are called "honorable" and even "most honorable" have no sympathy for the oppressed and certainly no desire to change things in the garrisons. The lust for power is so great, that even modern-day slavery which long ago became a feature of some garrisons, remains entrenched in Jamaica today!

Coincidentally too, Jamaica has more churches per square mile than any other nation in the world, which could indicate to the outside world that we have strong moral leadership here.

Clearly however, the Jamaican brand of "Christianity" finds modern-day slavery, garrison politics and rampant criminality quite compatible with their religion. For I cannot recall ever hearing any of our church leaders making it their mission to help free our modern-day slaves, unlike some outstanding white church leaders during the trans-Atlantic slave trade!

And even when three government ministers Dr. Peter Phillips, Dr. Omar Davies and Dr. Carl Blythe, openly displayed that their allegiance to the slain don Willie Haggart was more important than matters of state, the churches found that quite Christ-like as there was nary a word of condemnation from them! Clearly "our good men of the cloth" do not share Edmund Burke's view that;

"The only thing necessary for the triumph of evil is for good men to do nothing."

But let me back up.

I had only come to know about Haggart a few months before. I had been driving down Maxfield Avenue, a major corridor in Kingston which passes through the violent garrison constituencies of the former prime minster Portia Simpson Miller and her deputy, Dr. Peter Phillips. It was there I saw a convoy of about six or seven high end vehicles travelling slowly in the opposite direction. Since I had only seen this type of entourage when we had visiting dignitaries, I called a businessman in the area that I knew, to find out what was the special occasion.

He laughed at my naivety as he asked if I had not heard of Willie Haggart the powerful leader of the Black Roses Gang. According to him, that was how the notorious gangster travelled, for ever since he had stolen some US $20 million of cocaine money from his Colombian cohorts, they had put a contract on his head. By driving in a convoy, no one could tell which vehicle he was in and he laughed cynically as he revealed that most of the persons driving the vehicles in the convoy were policeman! To tell the truth, I was hardly surprised at this revelation, having long known of the very overt and tight links between members of the police force and some hoodlums.

When the news of that don's death came in April 2001, the senior government ministers immediately abandoned the people's business in parliament to hurry to the scene.

Even more shocking, Haggart's body was allowed to "lie in state" in our National Arena before his burial, an honor usually reserved for people who have given valuable service to the country!

This type of scenario would have been met with absolute horror by citizens of a civilized country, but in Jamaica, the reaction was muted so, is it any wonder that we just cannot progress?

The idea of *a child of the garrison* even thinking of playfully telling others to vote for the other side would most likely have been considered a capital offence in those criminal areas which flourish with full endorsement of their "elected" representatives" therefore.

That is why every time I remember the conversation with Miss Knight, I thank my lucky stars that I was born in a rural community and not one of those enclaves!

The thing is, I really did not have much exposure or interest in politics growing up, and had believed we practiced the "Westminster Model," which is one of the most stable forms of democracy in the world. I just did not until the 70's, know anything about cultism and the widespread acceptance of this distortion of our democratic process through the establishment and maintenance of garrison constituencies by the JLP and PNP.

Of course, when I was in the PNP, I had heard about the "evil empire" in Tivoli Gardens, but never of Matthews Lane. Neither did I realize how much the PNP admired the Tivoli model nor how much they wished to perfect and expand the system, until Spaulding put his plans into action!

The fact that I am able to cite far more examples of the PNP's overt association/protection of the political gangsters, has nothing to do with any personal bias but rather because the PNP now operates far more garrison constituencies than the JLP. Further with the PNP being in power for over 30 of the fifty odd years of our independence, their affiliated gangsters tend to be far more prosperous and high profile!

Looking back now, I am not sure that if I had been exposed to these things, I would have been swayed by even the great communicator Michael Manley, to return to Jamaica, much less to get involved in political activity.

Maybe, in retrospect however, I should have realized that Jamaican politics was not kosher!

For when I was around 9 years old, I was involved in an incident which should have led me to totally dislike politics and stay as far as possible from politicians.

My mother having been a highly respected social activist and Justice of Peace was often recruited to act as a Returning Officer (a non- political local administrator for the Electoral Office) each election day. I recall that in one particular election, the JLP candidate was a white property owner named Spencer Hendricks who ran against the incumbent, never-losing PNP candidate B. B. Coke. Hendricks became the Custos of St. Elizabeth many years later.

I do not recall if I had visited the office during that voting period because I had to take something for my mom or just went to where she was out of curiosity. Anyway, driven by prankishness, I took the opportunity to dip my finger into the bottle of indelible ink that voters are required to stain their fingers with, to show they had already voted. I then escaped downstairs to triumphantly tell all who would listen (the voting station was above the Malvern Police station) that I had voted.

I did not know that anyone took me seriously until sometime later when Spencer Hendricks arrived there and I heard him shouting to someone to "lock her up." It didn't take very long for me to realize that he was shouting at a policeman and that the "her" he was referring to, was me! For it had been reported to him by one of his supporters that I had really voted and because my parents were known to be supporters of the PNP, he assumed that my "voting" would not have benefited him.

Man was I ever scared when I discerned what was really happening, for I was born claustrophobic so images of being locked up and having to spend the rest of my life behind bars, became graphic, terrifying and real in my mind.

Despite my protestations that I was only joking and had not really voted, he remained loud and insistent. I don't recall how long the scenario lasted but all I can remember is that I was extremely scared at the thought of being locked up. For I could see that Hendricks was out for blood and even when other supporters of his joined in telling him that I was just a child and it was not true that I voted, he remained angry and resolute.

Luckily for me, the headmistress of the infant school I had attended, a Mrs. Fraser-Davis who had been the JLP's Indoor Agent in the polling station, and whose duty it was to ensure that everything went well from her party's stand point, heard the commotion and came downstairs. When she saw what was happening, she calmly verified that that I had not indeed voted but had simply dipped my finger in the ink and run out.

Only then could I breathe again.

I don't think I ever entered a polling station after that and since the voting age was then 21 years, I never even considered voting or having anything to do with politics, up to when I migrated to Canada and the USA.

When my then husband and I went to New York to live, it was during the civil rights riots there and although it was not party politics but rather the politics of race that was being played out there, my heart immediately warmed to the Black Panthers and Malcolm X. For in my book, the only way black people could get any justice in that country was to overthrow the white regime by force.

Anyway, I did not stay in the USA long enough to get involved in any form of activism as when I was there it was winter time and I was not inclined to venture outside unless it was an emergency, which in my book, the demonstrations weren't. In addition, we did not like New York so after about six months there we decided to live in Canada where we had far more relatives.

There we found no racial turmoil then, because the Canadians were just too polite to let it be known if they had a bias against blacks. So, although I kept a listening ear to what was happening in the USA, that was as far as my interest in politics went until the great communicator, the articulate Michael Manley, leader of the opposition in Jamaica and son of the founder of the PNP, visited Canada.

One of his speaking engagements took him to the Jamaica-Canadian Association an organization in which

a relative of ours, the late J.B. Campbell, had been a founding member. He served the organization for many years in several executive positions and constantly ensured that we attended important functions there.

While delivering his message, Manley painted such a graphic picture of poverty and deprivation in Jamaica and spoke so feelingly of the wickedness and oppression being meted out to the people by the JLP government, that my heart bled.

For growing up in the country, while there were poor people around, everyone had some land and a home no matter how humble. I had therefore never been exposed to zinc fences, lack of water and toilets and the general terrible conditions he described as being prevalent in the inner-cities at home.

In fact, at that time, I did not even know that Jamaica had ghettos! For I recall clearly, visiting Panama shortly after and being shocked at the horrible shanty towns in a section of

Colon and even declaring that people did not have to put up with such terrible living conditions at home!

Truth is I really did not know at that time that we had places far worse than that in my own island, for as a country-girl I never really had reason to go into the areas that Manley spoke so feelingly about.

So, when he exhorted us to get involved in getting rid of the wicked government at home and helping the poor, ending "You must come home to build your country," you know who was ready to board the next flight! For he had outlined such misery at home that only one without a social conscience could have ignored his pleas for help.

I think four of us, (my ex and I and two friends) who heard him that day, decided right away to return home and help "liberate the poor and dispossessed" but the other two returned to Canada within a few years.

Anyway besides pricking my social conscience, I just needed an excuse to go home for I realized very early that the cold weather in Canada was just not made for me and besides, at that time, I could not easily get Jamaican fruits and foods in Toronto, so I was feeling quite deprived!

The Long Way Home

Once my ex-husband and I decided to return home, we agreed to take the long way by road via North, Central and South America. This was at a time when the Pan American Highway was just about to be completed, running from the United States to Panama.

As we had recently bought a cute little convertible MG Midget sports car so we could really enjoy the limited summer sunshine in Toronto, we decided to take it home as Jamaica has year-round sunshine to enjoy.

We mapped a route through interesting cities in the USA then on down the Pan American Highway to Panama from where we would ship the car to Jamaica and continue our tour of the Americas by going down the magnificent Amazon River by boat. We did not give ourselves a time table but decided that if we liked a particular place, we would hang around there for a while and where we didn't, we would move on.

So, packing a sleeping bag, a camping stove, a minimum of clothes and a tent, we set off with our map on the road trip of our lives.

I think it was sometime in September that we set out and unfortunately as we never had blogs in those days, I did not record what turned out to be the most exciting tour I ever embarked upon. However, some experiences remain indelibly etched in my memory.

The first challenging experience I recall was being awakened by freezing weather in the middle of the night as we camped somewhere in Ohio. In fact, just writing about it now, made me re-live the biting cold that had crept into our tent and sleeping bag causing us to have to jump up quickly, pack up our equipment and take off in the middle of the night.

It seemed the snow had been determined to follow us too for the only problem we ever had with our wonderful car was a puncture just outside Dallas, Texas. And guess what, as we started to fix it, down came snow and we later learnt that it was the first time in about forty years that snow had fallen in that area so early.

And how can I forget my first exposure to gambling?

There we were in Las Vegas with the bright lights, fantastic shows, an air of excitement at every turn and best of all, the sound of money clinking from machines all around us. We were overwhelmed by the sheer ambiance of the place but had been *initially,* conscious enough to store our money in our tent and had only taken a few dollars into the casino.

Problem was, what we took with us went very quickly. I remember winning a pile of quarters and thinking this was going to be my fate for the rest of the night, put it all back.

There is something about Las Vegas and the atmosphere there that seems to seize one's good sense, for stupidly we went back and raided our tent of all our savings and headed back to the casinos. I don't have to tell you that we lost almost all our cash for when we left the casinos, we barely had enough money left to buy gas to go to California.

We therefore went back to our abode, packed up our camping equipment and high-tailed it out of that desert.

I guess it is true that out of evil comes good for that experience surely cured me of giving in to the lure of gambling forever. For although I have been back to Las Vegas quite a few times since then as I love the ambiance and the shows, have visited other casinos numerous times in far flung places such as the Bahamas, Germany, St. Martin, St. Kitts,

Monaco, Antigua and Atlantic City, I now only go to enjoy the entertainment but never take more than a maximum $ 10 with me into any of the casinos and when it is done it is done!

Anyway, back to the trip.

The next stop was California where we were going to have to work to earn back some money to keep on travelling.

Luckily, before I migrated from Jamaica, I had learnt to use something called a "unit record machine." For the benefit of the young, this machine was the precursor to the computer which some people today, think has been around forever!

The unit record machine read data stored on cards. The machine read the data by identifying the information punched in holes. The "intelligent" section of that machine was the huge metal panels with strings. I had learnt to punch the cards and configure the panels before I migrated.

When I went to Canada to live and study, as computers were in operation there and there was a great demand for computer programmers that is what I studied for because of the shortage of skilled persons in that profession, the money one could earn was really phenomenal. This was in the late 60's when a computer was the size of a large room and everything was stored on huge reel-to-reel tapes.

When we went to California, realizing that to get a job as a programmer would require me having to make a long term commitment; I opted instead to go back to my original training in key punching. This being a transient occupation with people going in and out of such jobs on a regular basis, it was consequently quite easy to gain employment for a few weeks.

We settled for Los Angeles where we found a cheap hotel on Hollywood Boulevard. And that was quite a surprise for I had always thought of Hollywood Boulevard as being glitzy. Yes, it is in parts, but it is an extremely long road and there are sections that are really run down. It was in the run-down area that we found a hotel we could afford. But it was no big thing for having lived in a tent for weeks that was quite a step-up in life.

We stayed in LA for around six weeks and we did not just work and save but toured the state extensively on weekends. It is from that time that I decided that my favorite city in North America was San Francisco, even though it gets extremely cold and breezy at times.

When we left, we headed south towards Mexico. I recall how difficult it was to cross from San Diego over to Tijuana for although our papers were all in good order, immigration kept sending us back. It took us several trips back and forth to the USA before we understood that all they wanted to let us in was a bribe of a couple US dollars!

We got a far better reception in Guadalajara though, because as we drove into the town, we saw a group of young people around our age in an American convertible car drawing up beside us. I suspect it was our Ontario license plate which had attracted them, so they welcomed us profusely to their country. After that reception, we became instant friends and for as long as we stayed there, they took us partying, to the beaches, introduced us to tequila and their marijuana, which they claimed was better than Jamaican *ganja.*

I had never seen ganja in Jamaica much less used it, so I could not compare. For growing up in the country, we had been told that it was only mad people who used ganja. To reinforce the story, all the crazy people we saw walking the streets in those days, were pointed out as ganja users!

I recall though not liking the taste at all as the *spliff* (small marijuana cigarette) I got to share was so tiny that it burnt my lip. It must have been quite a burn too as I can still feel the pain! Anyway, I found tequila a better bet.

Problem was it crept upon me. For while I was drinking it at a party and sitting down, I was telling my new found friends that is was ineffective and nothing close to our Jamaican rum. I am however still embarrassed to confess that the minute I stood up I fell flat on my face on the ground. How can I ever forget such a memorable event?

We had a wonderful time hanging out with our new found friends. When we were ready to move on, they warned us about camping anywhere in Central America for they said there were two legged and four legged predators and snakes all around.

I remember when we got a couple miles out of Mexico City; it was nightfall so we decided to sleep in the car as we thought it would be too difficult to go hotel hunting in the night. Well I have news for you for when a cold spell, arrives you do anything to survive.

55

With Mexico City being over seven thousand feet above sea level, it is freezing in the nights. So, we had to turn on the heater and start driving into the city to find a hotel that night.

Mexico City was quite wonderful so we tarried there for quite a while, travelling all over during the day. I can never forget the first day when we drove away from our hotel to explore, but amazingly, forgot to write down the name of the hotel and the street it was on.

Luckily, we had marked the location on the map and when night caught up with us, we stopped under a street light to try and find out where we were and where our hotel was. We were getting nowhere fast though.

Soon we were approached by a very angry policeman for it turned out we had stopped right under a "no stopping" sign! I had not seen the sign although I had been able to get around Mexico quite all right as my Spanish was reasonable.

When Spanish speakers are angry though, they speak very rapidly and even now, I cannot understand a word under such circumstances. However, it did not take him long to realize that his anger was being wasted because I had long lost track of what he was saying and I guess, was gaping like a big dummy.

When he discovered we were strangers and lost, his entire attitude changed. He shook his head in amazement when we told him that we did not know the name of the hotel we were staying at as we had failed to write it down. However, he was able to quickly tell us the name on seeing where it had been marked on the map. Once he found it, he told us to follow him, jumped on his bike with siren blaring and led us home. And he did not want any money for helping us either. I am sorry we never got his name for I can never forget that cop as even now, I still feel a lot of gratitude to him.

The only thing I regret about that visit to Mexico was eating lizard. For there is nothing I hate more than that reptile, but having been encouraged by our hosts in Guadalajara to try a new dish, I did and it was surely delicious.

Then I discovered it was Iguana and got very sick as I kept picturing a lizard moving around in my stomach! I also found it really scary as we drove around in our convertible, seeing kids on the roadside advertising their iguanas for sale by swinging them in the air by the rope that they had used to tie their legs. Just remembering that sight, still makes my skin crawl.

And talking about food reminds me how much I had come to love burritos while working in California. I could therefore hardly wait to get to Mexico where I thought I would be able to eat lots of "the real macoy" ie. authentic burritos. I noticed however, that whenever I asked for a burrito at a restaurant, I would get a very strange look. Then while spending some time in a remote village, I can't recall the name, I again asked for burritos. This time my request was met with hearty laughter. For according to those villagers, a burrito was a small donkey and they did not eat donkeys there.

That made me wonder if the (Mexican?) inventor of this tasty treat had so named it to play a trick on naive Americans for I got the impression it was concocted in the USA but was totally unknown in Mexico in the early 70's!

Anyway, on that trip I did develop such a great love for Mexico and the Mexican people that it has caused me to visit that country several times since then.

Guatemala was a different ballgame as it was then a place of *bribes* for it was under martial law. So, it felt like every mile we drove, we were stopped by fierce looking soldiers with automatic rifles, who it turned out just wanted some Yankee dollars. No wonder I cannot remember anything about our time there, but I do not think we tarried there at all that time. I have been there since then to cover an election and found the country delightful on that subsequent trip.

However, we did tarry in El Salvador during the road trip. This is because we got such a warm reception there. I don't recall if we went to other towns in that country but I can never forget the fun we had at the hotel in the capital, San Salvador.

When we were checking in and showed our passports as required, the clerk had asked us where Jamaica was. In those days, the legendary Bob Marley had not yet had the international impact he now has which had helped put us on the map worldwide. Neither had we yet produced an Usain Bolt who is now known everywhere as the fastest man on the planet, so their lack of knowledge about our influential little island was understandable.

Our neighbor Cuba was however very dominant in the region at that time as the extremely popular revolutionary, Che Guevara had been assassinated in Bolivia just a few years before. He was at the time being heralded as the hero of Spanish America. So, we explained to the clerk that Jamaica was an island *next door* to Cuba.

This was understandable in the 70's, but would you believe that despite our music rocking the world for decades and our sportsmen and women thrilling sports fans world-wide, I was asked the same question "Where is Jamaica" in 2015?

This was in New Mexico so since I figured that the gentleman who asked me the question could not be either a music or sports fan, I gave him the same answer I had given the hotel clerk in El Salvador over three decades ago, although I had long thought I would never ever have had to give that description again in my life.

Anyway, in El Salvador at that time, that was our instant passport to great treatment. I do not remember if it was on a national holiday when we arrived but there was a big party in the hotel that night. We were pleasantly surprised when during the festivities the master of ceremonies kept calling on us to stand up as he introduced us to great applause, as the *"Amigos from Jamaica."* Every time he mentioned Jamaica however, he stressed that it was located beside Cuba. It was absolutely overwhelming. And that is all I can remember about our stay in El Salvador!

I recall though how backward Honduras was at that time so we never tarried there at all, just basically passed though. For we had found it discomforting that at the border with Guatemala at the immigration office, they were using kerosene lamps, as electricity was not very widespread in that country at that time, we were told.

Next it was on to Nicaragua and my starkest memories of that country are of Lake Nicaragua and the ominous looking Arenal Volcano. Arenal is in the northern section of Costa Rica, but it is so huge and sinister- looking, that it appears to tower over the entire southern section of Nicaragua.

I remember how as we drove away from it, it seemed to be following us threateningly with what appeared to be permanent smoke hovering over the peak. Since it had erupted in 1968 after being dormant for decades, I had felt especially scared. I have however visited the beautiful spa below it since then, and found the various degrees of warm water which fill the baths, absolutely invigorating and felt no way threatened anymore.

As I now write, I regret not having gone over to Bluefields in Nicaragua when I was there. For that area is named after a lovely beach that we have in western Jamaica. I recall hearing many years ago that Bluefields in Nicaragua was mainly populated by Jamaican immigrants. According to the information, when some of the thousands of Jamaicans who had gone to work on the Panama Canal in the early 1900's, completed their duties there, instead of returning home, a significant number had headed north to the Caribbean coasts of Nicaragua and Costa Rica.

I actually have quite close relatives living in Bluefields for I remember when I was quite young; I met two young cousins from that area. They had come to Jamaica to live with a relative who operated a bakery in the small town of Chapleton in the mid-island parish of Clarendon, in order to learn English. Problem is, in such deep rural areas in Jamaica, English is *not* generally spoken! So, when it was discovered that they were only becoming fluent in Jamaican curse words and the local lingo, patois, they were quickly packed up and sent back home.

Interestingly it seems Jamaican curse words are a favorite among Spanish speaking descendants of Jamaican immigrants in Central America. For I remember on that same trip, hearing two kids cursing on top of their voices in Colon, Panama and when we thought they were Jamaicans and started to talk to them, they turned out to be born Panamanians who did not know a word of English or even patois, but were fluent in our curse words! I have also encountered similar situations in Limon in Costa Rica.

Anyway, as far as my long lost cousins in Bluefields were concerned, in retrospect, I would have had no way of finding them as I don't even remember their names. It would have been nice to visit the area though to see what it was like but it is not too late is it?

I stray.

It was on that road trip that I really fell in love with Costa Rica, which still remains one of the few countries I tell myself I would live in, if I ever leave Jamaica. What I really loved about that country from day one was its lushness, the beaches on the Caribbean coast and mountains. I have visited it four times since then and have always found it wonderful.

We had a memorable time in Panama partly because that is
where we met a very pleasant San Blas Indian named John
who seemed anxious to adopt us. We had shipped our car to
Jamaica from Panama and were checking how best to go into
South America by boat.

John worked in the canal-zone and spoke his native language
plus English and Spanish fluently. I don't remember exactly
how we met him. But maybe we encountered him while we
were trying to get on the boat to visit the islands on our own,
for I do recall we were having a language problem with the
captain. In retrospect,

I remember clearly now that *it was* John who convinced the
captain to take us on as passengers. For the boats that went to
those islands from Colon at the time were cooperatively
owned by the Indians. They were used mainly to transport
their people and food and I recollect that they were totally
against taking foreigners on as passengers.

The San Blas Islands are an archipelago comprising of 265
islands and cays but only 49 were inhabited. At that time,
those islands were being governed by Colombia and there was
conflict with Panama over whose jurisdiction they should
really fall under. The inhabitants, apart from those who
worked at the Canal Zone, had very little exposure to
outsiders except to fishermen and a few other persons coming
from Colombia and Panama.

It did not take me long to regret the decision to go to the
islands, for the trip over to the first island, which probably
lasted about three days in the small crowded boat, was so

rough and scary that I think I promised God that if I survived, I would return home and become a missionary.

I do not think I have ever vomited so much in my life and I remember the Indians passing around huge cups of coffee in the mornings and giving us dried bread for breakfast. Other meals were just rice but I don't recall being able to eat anything before we hit shore.

As we arrived at the first island, John introduced us to the chief and arranged for us to sleep in hammocks in the school. He accompanied us to several islands over the period we were there and made similar arrangements at all the islands that we visited.

The San Blas Indians were extremely tiny in stature and I recall some even marveling at how tall I was for a woman. I also remember there being an over-abundance of albinos on most of the islands we visited and John telling us that this was because there was a lot of inter- marriage.

The women wore beautifully hand-woven clothes like what you see in Guatemala but the men were very scantily dressed. I was only able to take one picture with them during the long period we were there however, as according to their folk-lore, when you photograph them, you stole their souls!

The buildings on all the islands we visited were made of thatch and sticks and the floors were simple warm, soft, white sand. These frail buildings were quite adequate on those islands however for although the islands are on the Caribbean coast of Panama; this region never has any hurricanes.

I don't think we would have left those islands for weeks as we were having such a wonderful time just hanging out on the cays and beaches, swimming and fishing.

Then, some nuns came over from Colombia to do health checks on the Indians. That was when we learnt that most of them suffered from tuberculosis.

That information of course caused instant panic for we had been freely sharing utensils and living really closely to them. (Months later after I had returned home and was having "morning sickness," not knowing the cause of my "illness," I swore I had contracted the disease. I only relaxed when the doctor assured me that what I was carrying was far more delightful, welcome and beautiful, as morning sickness is a common occurrence in pregnancy!)

Anyway, when the nuns broke the news, we never went back into a schoolroom or hut again but instead sat on the beach waiting for the first boat we could get to take us over to Colombia. I think it was about two days before we got a little canoe which a fisherman said we could travel in.

I will never forget that trip either as the engine of that boat kept shutting off and we could see the black fins of sharks swarming around, from time to time.

That boat went to a little fishing village named Macao, but unfortunately for us, we could not get to a proper town as there had been a huge land-slide blocking the access road. We eventually got a room to rent in a house with thatched roof and dirt floor and as there was no bathroom available, we used the sea for everything! I cannot recall how long we were there but finally a little plane came in, around a six-seater, and we were able to fly out. *Phew.*

I don't remember much else about our time in Colombia on that trip but after we left, we spent quite a few weeks with a relative, Uncle Joe, who lived in Venezuela.

He lived in Maracaibo the second largest city in the country after Caracas. It's famous for its culture, big shopping malls and beautiful parks and is called "La Primera Ciudad de Venezuela," (the Most Important Venezuelan City) because of its development. Uncle Joe worked in the oil industry there and really gave us a wonderful time taking us on tours and to restaurants all over.

Unfortunately, we were unable to go down the Amazon River as planned, for it was while we were in Venezuela that we met some backpackers from the Netherlands. They had just returned from Brazil and told us that they had heard that the last boat that went down the Amazon had been hijacked and the passengers' throats cut. At the time I had a really attractive throat which I valued greatly and decided that it was indeed time to head home.

Democratic Socialism, Hogwash and Hypocrisy

When I returned to Jamaica, I immediately jumped into political activity, joining the PNP Youth Organization (PNPYO), a party group in my area and later the PNP "Task Force" which was where one heard about the cushy jobs available in government service which they wanted to have filled with dedicated party people. You see, because of the socialist thrust of the party and the aim being to nationalize as many private enterprises and properties as possible, ideological purity had to be guaranteed.

I was soon to learn that it was not only the white-collar jobs that were given out to dedicated party people, for the victimization and exclusion of non-PNP people was the accepted practice. So even the people cleaning the streets were generally only allowed to earn a small living if they were certified "socialists." Although I thought that was quite disgusting, I accepted the explanation that this was how things had been done under the JLP which had ruled the country since Independence, so by reserving *all* government jobs for PNP supporters, they were merely levelling the playing field.

As I write this, I am so ashamed at how eagerly I swallowed the justification of a terrible practice that has brought so much grief to the country. Especially after Manley had come to Canada and encouraged us to return home and help clean up corruption.

Because then, he had emphasized that victimization on the basis of politics was one of the evils the JLP government had been practicing and it was something *his* government would never tolerate.

But I was too much in awe of Manley at the time to recognize immediately that his adoption of the same "evil" he condemned, was the first sign of the type of debilitating hypocrisy for which he later became so notorious.

The thing I really looked forward to in terms of political activism however was joining in street demonstrations which were in vogue in those days. The two issues I remember most clearly, which gave us reason to hit the streets regularly were; the fact that persons under age 21 could not vote and the "sinful" lottery that the government operated.

At that time, the propaganda that caught the public's imagination declared that because Jamaica was a Christian country, it was sinful for the government to operate a lottery. This found resonance with the churches many of whose leaders never missed an opportunity to remind their congregations how evil gambling was. This, even though the profits from the lottery were then being used to upgrade the health sector, a sector that has always badly needed funds to raise the level of service for those who are poor and sick.

Most churches in Kingston however dived into this issue and the executive and members of the Jamaica Council of Churches (JCC) were forefront in participating in the regular demonstrations, impressively decked out in their religious garb.

On my return too, I had become so fanatical, that anything Manley even suggested, I obeyed unthinkingly. So, when he exhorted us to shun foreign products and told us to *eat Jamaican*, I immediately started eating and drinking everything local, throwing out things like even good Canadian whiskey (rye) for which I had developed a liking.

This naïve stance of mine continued until I realized that what the leadership of the PNP was telling us was sheer, unadulterated hogwash and hypocrisy. For while they encouraged Jamaicans to eat local, they were indulging themselves with every foreign luxury.

This I found out soon after, on attending a party a minister hosted for his girlfriend and seeing champagne and caviar flowing freely!

It was that type of *double speak* that I noticed in the PNP that soon caused me to start shedding the scales from my eyes, thank God.

My flirtation with the PNP lasted for about four years after I had returned to Jamaica in 1971, and had eagerly and unthinkingly embraced "Democratic Socialism."

I soon recognized however that the democratic label was all a sham, for a large influential arm of the party was not at all interested in social justice for all. They were instead being driven by deep resentment against the more affluent members of the society and a lust for supreme power. Being in influential positions in the party did give them the opportunity to grab immense wealth for themselves, using friends, family and political cohorts who they put into strategic positions, to rape the public enterprises that had been nationalized.

Having been exposed to Fidel Castro, the powerful leader in Cuba, and the supreme power he could wield unhampered in his island, they consequently saw pressing on to full communism as the best vehicle to total power and glory for themselves.

They also found a willing ally in Jamaica in the Worker's Party of Jamaica (WPJ), founded and led by Dr. Trevor Munroe, a lecturer at the University of the West Indies, (then our only university) which it was alleged at the time, financed its weapon purchases and other activities by carrying out bank robberies.

Because Jamaicans were at that time generally kind and caring people, which is what the democratic socialist package at first implied it would promote, (social justice,) Manley's initial message got overwhelming support from almost every sector in the entire nation.

What Manley did not take into consideration however was the fact that because we were close to both Cuba and America, the general population was totally exposed to both systems of government. So, when he tried to *surreptitiously* introduce Cuban style totalitarianism into Jamaica, the direct threat this would pose to press freedom and the democratic process to which we were accustomed, was immediately exposed and resisted.

The Cuba and Russia of the 70's

For the benefit of those born after the 80's, I must reiterate that Cuba and Russia are not *today* what they were then.

During that period, the USSR Empire which was dominated by Russia was extremely powerful with numerous satellite-states worldwide which were controlled and dominated by the huge USSR military machine and the KGB. And they had no reservations about foisting their totalitarian system on other countries, using the bullet whenever and wherever they could get a toehold.

Cuba, as its regional satellite saw the small vulnerable Caribbean islands as easy pickings, especially if it could get influential people and an organization like Manley's PNP, the WPJ and the New Jewel Movement in Grenada, to become their surrogates and open the doors.

As the Jamaican proxies drew closer to the Cubans, numerous Cuban soldiers were deployed into Jamaica (and Grenada as well, we later learnt) and spread out under the guise that they were building mini-dams and schools.

In Jamaica, they also recruited young men who were sent to Cuba, supposedly to be trained in work-related skills. Instead they were trained in guerilla warfare. One defector from the program exposed it all in a book published in the 70's called "The Road Not Taken."

The Cuban assistance to the PNP did not stop there however as that country also provided wanted PNP gunmen with a safe haven in which to remain until the heat had worn off. A typical example of this was the Tony Brown /George Flash affair to which I referred to earlier.

It was only after the Berlin wall was torn down through the efforts of Presidents Reagan and Mikael Gorbachev in 1989 and the USSR disintegrated, that Cuba's financial and military sponsorship was cut drastically and they had to reduce their activities in the Caribbean.

As Cuba became less threatening to the small, vulnerable Caribbean countries, attitudes towards them thawed to the point that in 1998, Edward Seaga, Jamaica's foremost anti-communist leader in the 70's and a former prime minister, even met with Castro when he came on an official visit to Jamaica. He then declared;

> *"We made it quite clear that those days (the 70's) are behind us. We are not dealing with memories; we are dealing with the future."*

So. if one looks at the activities of the Cubans during the 70's and 80's through today's eyes after the general thaw and after USA started to re-establish relations with Cuba, one could never understand the dynamics we had to deal with and pressures that freedom-loving Jamaicans faced during the Manley years before he was booted out of power in 1980 and kept at bay until 1989.

In the mid-seventies the Cuban presence was extremely intimidating, as hordes of Cuban young men were ever-present, threateningly traversing our streets in open-back trucks. Many of us who were not prepared to give up our freedoms and the democratic way of life to which we had been born, soon started to openly criticize their presence and actions, for it was a matter of *death before dishonor* for us.

This caused their ambassador to Jamaica (who was suspected to also be the head of the Cuban DGI intelligence agency assigned to Jamaica,) Ulysses Estrada, a former General in the Cuban army, to be brazen enough to deliver a message in person on our government-owned television station, (clearly, with the full permission and endorsement of the Manley government) menacingly stating that if we did not stop criticizing his country and people, he would bring his troops into Jamaica to "...deal with us!"

That period did not only threaten our freedoms, but also our possessions and sanity as well. For an integral part of the dangerous rhetoric that was driving fear into our hearts was the open promotion of stealing, of not only farmer's crops and people's private possessions but also land.

This was being encouraged by senior persons in the ruling party who sought *to sanitize theft* by calling it *"capturing."*

Those of us who were involved in farming were quickly targeted by people brazenly invading our property and saying they were "capturing" our things or our land "...as yu have plenty an wi nuh hab nun". (You have plenty and we have nothing). It was not just stealing from "wicked capitalists" that was encouraged either but also even verbal abuse and intimidation on the streets became commonplace. I personally was often verbally abused in traffic for being a "wicked rapacious capitalist," simply because I drove a car!

Even nastiness and a rejection of pride in one's surroundings were being promoted as the norm at that time by some in the hierarchy of the party.

For how can we ever forget that notorious, memorable and highly publicized event when Dr. D. K. Duncan, then Minister of Mobilization and General Secretary of the PNP, was invited to formally declare open a new German Automotive School that was built in his constituency to train young people, a gift from the German people? There he took the grand opportunity to criticize the gift by telling his audience, made up mainly of vulnerable young people, that the new building was too clean and should be "de-sanitized and demystified" so they could feel comfortable!

Any thought of the young people being exhorted to keep their new school clean was rejected as elitist and out of hand, as during that period, anti-social attitudes were being promoted by the hierarchy of the socialist movement and the messages being conveyed to the masses were being eagerly absorbed by the unthinking "lumpen." (The educated leaders of the communist/socialist movement openly and disparagingly referred to those who were not clever or well educated, as the lumpen, the shortened version of the Marxist term "lumpen proletariat.")

It was around that time that the late journalist/talk show host, Wilmot "Motty" Perkins declared in one of his regular columns;

> "........some of the harmful attitudes and practices being encouraged by the leaders will cause problems for at least a generation....."

However, although a generation has long passed, (a generation being 30 years) praedial larceny which stemmed from it being sanitized as "capturing" in the 70's, still remains the biggest problem for farmers today. And the dirtying up of our environment is turning Jamaica into a big garbage dump. I really do not see any of these anti-social actions being reversed any time soon either.

For when the seeds of freeness and carelessness were planted, implying that; what others had should be "shared" with lazy and unproductive persons; nothing was wrong with capturing; dirty was good and clean should be disregarded as it was elitist; such messages were eagerly absorbed by susceptible minds and have become entrenched and remain an integral part of our present culture.

With violence based on political animosities increasing and destructive rhetoric being tossed around at persons you were non-socialists, it was only a matter of time before even those with only little resources but lots of ambition, initiative and skill, joined their wealthier counterparts by migrating from Jamaica in droves, taking their assets and skills with them.

As the cold war rhetoric inspired by obedience to Russia/Cuba escalated, it also targeted visitors to our island especially the "American imperialists" who made up 75% of our tourists, so it was not surprising that during that socialist experiment, tourism floundered, our GDP reduced sharply and increasingly, hard currency became scarce.

While the apologists for the Manley regime love to blame the economic decline in the 70's on "destabilization by the CIA and local capitalists," nothing could be further from the truth.

According to noted Jamaican economist, Peter Blair Henry, Dean of New York University's Stern School of Business in his well-researched book "Turn Around" which was written in 2013, it was the *management* of the economy by the Manley regime which led to our economic demise.

In this easy to read but highly rated publication, Henry compared the performance of the Jamaican and Barbadian economies, as both countries are; former colonies of Britain; shared an almost identical history and were equally affected by international shocks such as the oil price increases in the 70's.

In 2012, the per capita GDP in Barbados was $14,498 while Jamaica struggled at the bottom with a GDP of $5,275. According to the CIA Fact Book, in 2014 the GDP had risen to $16,200 in Barbados and ours to a mere $8,700. Interestingly at the same time it was $25,100 in the Bahamas, another country with a similar history as ours.

But back to our particular tribulations in the 70's.

It was therefore only a matter of time before the shortage of all basic imported goods set in. It was these shortages which led to the burgeoning of a new group of entrepreneurs called Informal Commercial Importers, (ICI's). These were enterprising, mostly women, who saw an opportunity to make a quick buck by taking farm products abroad to places like Cayman Islands, sell them and use the hard currency to purchase and bring back scarce products for the Jamaican consumer.

While they were embraced at first, when they started to "marry" their products, this caused a great deal of distress and annoyance. For if one wanted to buy a scarce basic food item like rice, it was often "married" to things like sanitary napkins, condoms and other non- essentials with wider profit margins, thus putting a grave burden on the poor and middle class.

By 1977, the lack of foreign exchange caused by the careless financial management of the Manley government; the bleeding of privatized entities by supporters who had been installed to run them but who had neither the competence, inclination nor ability to run a business; rampant corruption including handouts to family and their supporters; led us to have to turn to the International Monetary fund, (IMF) with their well-known harsh "conditionalities," to survive.

Having the IMF around did provide some comic relief for those of us on the other side that enjoyed painting graffiti all over Kingston despite it being a dangerous exercise. For the initials IMF were soon translated to mean *IS MANLEY FAULT*, a slogan which featured prominently in all our propaganda material after that.

And I say painting graffiti was a dangerous exercise because I vividly recall the night, we were busy painting up the roads in Edgewater, in St. Catherine. As we "worked," a car with about four rough looking men screeched to a stop beside us and they demanded to know what we were doing. Scared out of our wits as we suspected they were armed, we couldn't say a word and seeing how frightened we were, they demanded that we immediately paint out the graffiti. That we quickly and sheepishly did as they stood aside, menacingly watching us. And we considered ourselves very lucky that night as the news was replete with reports of people being killed or seriously injured by both JLP and PNP gunmen, while carrying out similar peaceful political activities.

After that, we never went out to paint without having "lookout" people with CB radios, as there were no cell phones around then and that was the closest thing we had to instant communication.

I remember all too well too, the frequent power cuts during that dark era, as the government could not afford to buy even oil, to keep the generators at the publicly- owned power company rolling, due to a shortage of foreign exchange. I also remember having to line up on alternating days to be allowed the *luxury* of buying fuel for my vehicle and of course lining up to buy basic foods.

There was an experience I had one day while lining up to buy a loaf of bread in a supermarket, which I can never forget.

Although I now relate it as a joke, it was not at all funny at the time. I had been at the supermarket when the word went out that a bread delivery van had arrived to replenish the empty shelves. As I had two young children at home who just loved bread, like everyone else in the store, I quickly jumped in line to get a loaf of the precious commodity.

After waiting for almost a half hour, I was finally handed a loaf, but suddenly, before I even knew what was happening, a hand appeared out of the blue and grabbed the "valuable" item from me. I had no clue where that hand came from and I never saw my bread again. Worse, although I quickly tried to get another loaf, by then the stock had totally disappeared and

I left that day, vowing never ever to line up again for anything.

As it turned out however, whoever said "Out of evil cometh good" was dead right. For during that period of shortages, I learnt to stop using things like sugar, flour and butter, which were all extremely scarce in those days. And now scientists and nutritionists are constantly declaring that frequent use of these products is very hazardous to one's health!

However, let me back up a bit; before we went for financial assistance to the IMF because of the scarcity of foreign exchange, it wasn't only the food shortages and verbal vitriol which escalated at that time but so did the violence. For skirmishes in the streets by supporters of the two dominant parties had become commonplace and the prevailing death and injury from the confrontations, made the daily news extremely alarming.

Soon this escalated into a fully blown undeclared civil war between PNP and JLP supporters who had long graduated from stones, knives and handguns to AK 47's, Uzis and M16's, allegedly supplied to the PNP by the Cuban DGI and Russian KGB and to the JLP by the American CIA.

I had become totally disenchanted with the PNP government by about early to mid-1975, but because I did not like what I heard about Edward Seaga, the fairly new leader of the JLP, I looked on from the sidelines. For, according to everyone who knew him, he was cold and dictatorial. This was the very opposite of the charismatic Michael Manley who was warm and at least pretended to be interested in the views of young people. I could therefore not contemplate supporting the JLP, so once again turned my back on politics.

I was then living in one of Kingston's dormitory communities "over the water" in St. Catherine called Edgewater. When the 1976 elections were approaching, Manley carried out the most dangerous and oppressive act that showed us that he was definitely attempting to give himself supreme power and become the Fidel Castro of Jamaica.

The Political State of Emergency

As people became more desperate over the deteriorating economic conditions, uncontrollable violence, financial constraints and shortages, the government responded with repression.

On Saturday 19th June, 1976, Manley declared that his government would be implementing a State of Emergency, with the reasons stated being:

(a) *To reduce crime and to apprehend the gunmen and the new breed of terrorist;*

(b) *To smash the link between politics and violence;*

(c) *To give the nation a breathing space to return to normality;*

(d) *To create an atmosphere of security conducive to the effective functioning of the economy;*

(e) *To permit Law abiding citizens comprising the overwhelming majority of our population, to pursue without fear their peaceable business in homes, work- places or in the streets and public places.*

(Source: National Library of Jamaica.)

While all that sounded lofty enough, instead of the State of Emergency being used as stated, it became an instrument to lock up influential opposition activists.

For, the then Minister of Security Keble Munn, immediately signed *blank* detention orders and gave them to their politically-aligned police, to at once arrest known JLP leaders and supporters all over the island. Those detained were then herded into cramped detention centers under the most inhumane conditions.

But not only were political adherents being arrested without charge but also it was often reported that police who had personal beefs against individuals, used their blank detention orders to deal with those issues too!

The real political intent of the state of emergency by the Manley government was strikingly and blatantly demonstrated by the detention of Karram Josephs, the JLP caretaker for probably, the most peaceful constituency in the island, on Election Day 1976.

This was in the rural constituency of North East Westmoreland where not one shot had been fired during the period. Josephs was locked up at 7 am on Election morning because he was said to be a threat to national security. Amazingly, this threat to national security disappeared at 6 pm that same evening after the polls had closed, so he was released!

Manley had insisted at the time that 1976 State of Emergency was declared that it was the government's initiative to deal with the escalation in violence, as recommended by his security advisors. That was soon exposed as a flagrant lie. For during a subsequent Commission of Enquiry held in 1978 and chaired by the then Chief Justice of Jamaica Justice Kenneth Smith, it was revealed that;

> "...... its calling was predicated upon the facilitation of political opportunism and not bona fide concerns about national security." The Smith Commission also found that the head of both intelligence agencies of government -- the Special Branch of the police force and the Military Intelligence Unit (MIU) of the Jamaica Defense Force -- never advised Manley of any potential threat to national security during Carifesta and, indeed, Deputy Commissioner Curtis Griffiths, head of the Special Branch, testified to the commission that he knew nothing about the intention to declare a State of Emergency; he read of it in the press, although he was the chief intelligence officer of government. Captain Carl Marsh, in charge of the MIU also gave devastating testimony. He advised that there was no need for a State of Emergency."

(Those who are interested in the details can consult the archives at the Institute of Jamaica for the full report.)

After the State of Emergency was declared and I saw that it was nothing but a political tool to help Manley gain supreme power, I decided that despite what I had been hearing about Seaga's leadership style, because he was the leader of the only viable alternative party, I would have to join the JLP.

For Russian/Cuban domination of my country was totally unacceptable to me.

I therefore started to assist in any way I could, Harry Bent, the JLP representative who was running in my Edgewater constituency.

Incidentally, switching from PNP to JLP, again reminded me of how cultish even very educated persons were when it came to politics.

I had a very good friend at high school with whom I had reconnected in PNPYO. (This was the youth wing of the PNP.) We then started to travel together, all over to the PNP meetings and collaborated closely on most things, not only political but private matters as well. I was therefore really shocked at how he took my change of sides for to me he was a friend.

Soon after it became known in party circles that I was campaigning for the JLP, I ran into him and hailed him up exuberantly. I can still see the raw hatred in his eyes as he glared at me, turned his back and walked away. He was at the time a lecturer at our only university (then), the University of the West Indies. His reaction really hurt me as I had considered him a true friend and not just a political associate.

I have had to eventually come to accept that this is how politics is practiced in Jamaica. In retrospect, I suppose I was lucky that I was only snubbed by my former friend, for in some areas, especially in the garrisons, openly changing party loyalty often led to one being assassinated!

The JLP had no chance of winning the 1976 general election because representatives, organizers and senior leaders such as Pernell Charles were being locked up and supporters were terrified that they could also be detained at any time. The memoirs of Charles" detention without charge are vividly recorded in his publication "**Detained.**"

After the 1976 election, the flight of citizens intensified. Many sold their properties for a song as by then, the government was threatening to escalate the nationalization of all assets, including private properties across the island.

Several large businesses and farms were also nationalized and turned into people's cooperatives with huge numbers of "socialists" settling on these as the proud new owners. In no time, the new owners sold off or devoured all the livestock and other farm products.

With no one replacing anything, the farms were soon left in ruins. Two very large and once ultra-productive farms, Nyerere and Hounslow come quickly to mind.

In addition to the nationalization drive, there was also increased *state terrorism* which further propelled the flight of the middleclass, business-persons and indeed anyone who could find a place of refuge or simply just leave Jamaica for anywhere. While some had become accustomed to being vilified on the streets as "rapacious capitalists" due to, for example, no other reason but owning and driving a motor vehicle, the escalating threats of physical violence or arrest without charge, became too much for them.

In the meantime, those intent on grabbing state power and resources soon became dissatisfied with using threats alone. So right after the 1976 election, actions designed to drive terror into the hearts of those refusing to endorse democratic socialism were put into place.

These included; the wide-scale burning down of the homes of dissenters; threats of detention under the State of Emergency and direct unprovoked acts of violence against innocent family members.

A friend who worked on the 1976 advertising & public relations campaign for the JLP, heard that he was down to be detained under the State of Emergency and fled to Canada. His adult daughter who had remained in Jamaica was subsequently kidnapped, raped by six men and left naked on Mona Road in Kingston which is near the University of the West Indies. Before they left her, the terrorists made sure to tell her why she had been chosen. I do not think he has been able to come to terms even now, with the fact that his daughter was savagely raped because he fled the clutches of the PNP.

Rape became widespread as a weapon to be used to terrorize, especially the middle class as they were the most publicly vocal against the Manley regime. Reports abounded about children, some as young as three years of age being raped. When the little girls could not be penetrated, knives were allegedly used to slit their vaginas open as their helpless parents were forced to watch, some horror stories revealed.

It was a terrible, chilling, dangerous and blood-curdling period and the outward flight of the middle class, professionals and entrepreneurs swelled to a deluge. Some streets in upper income areas were reportedly blocked by trailers as people hurried to flee the island with their families.

Some of today's millionaires and billionaires who were then members of, or relatives of members of the ruling political hierarchy that now dominate the island, got their start during that terrible, spine-tingling period by buying properties dirt-cheap or getting them free, when the owners hurriedly escaped to safer shores with their families.

During this period, most of the people I knew were completely panic-stricken. I think the only reason why we did not join the exodus is because we had only recently returned to Jamaica and had started to really explore this beautiful island of ours. We had bought a VW minibus and rigged it up with a play-pen and other child-friendly equipment so we could explore the island in comfort with our young children.

When we discovered that Jamaica was awash with beautiful natural features such as numerous rivers, waterfalls and lush mountains, far more beautiful than anything we had seen on our travels, we started to fully appreciate the treasure that was Jamaica.

Leaving it to be destroyed by political thugs therefore, was just not a palatable option for us.

At that time, I operated two lucrative children's nurseries, but longed to live on a farm in the country. We found a large rice farm in parish of St. Catherine (that parish is west of the capital) going for a bargain, so I sold my businesses and we jumped in head first. The former owner told us he was selling out cheap and migrating to Belize, the only English-speaking former British colony in Central America, because life in Jamaica had become too terrible.

During that period, there was rampant abuse of American tourists on our streets which caused the industry to nose-dive as the USA was, and still is our major tourism market. This along with the exodus of Jamaicans leaving and taking all their liquid assets with them heightened the chronic shortage of hard currency.

Under the increasing financial hardships, further repressive measures were legislated by the government, including them limiting Jamaicans traveling abroad, to obtaining a maximum of *US $50* to finance each trip!

That amount was stamped into one's passport and anyone found with more than the specified sum, would be immediately prosecuted by a newly established Financial Intelligence Unit (FIU) and given a mandatory jail sentence.

Incredibly, Montego Bay's most well-known and highly respected philanthropist, a Dr. Morrison who attempted to carry out additional funds to buy life-saving drugs (which were in short supply on the island), was one of the first persons jailed during that horrific period.

Meanwhile, just as they do today, the politicians shunned local medical services and would jump onto air ambulance and head to Miami when sick, with Jamaican taxpayers picking up the tab of course.

Agents from the FIU flooded airports during that time, supposedly to stem the outflow of hard currency. However, I was told by more than one person that *they* bribed officers from that same unit to take their money through all the security checks and return it to them once safely seated on the plane!

The farmer from whom we bought our property however, was clearly not into that racket. Faced with the futility of trying to buy tractor parts in Miami with just $50, he realized that very soon he would not have even $1 dollar to buy candy for his young kids when he travelled abroad, he had moaned. So, accepting that farming in Jamaica was on a downward spiral and he was moving full speed to possible ruin, he sold out and moved to Belize where land was virtually being given away to encourage farming.

The last I heard of him was that he was an extremely successful rice and orange farmer in Belize.

We paid down on his farm in St Catherine and moved in although we could scarcely afford the mortgage.

What we discovered on moving to the farm though was that although the area was mixed politically, it was predominantly PNP. Since we never hid our disgust with the government, we soon started to bleed financially because of our politics.

While my ex-husband concentrated on the rice side of things, my dream had always been to do livestock farming, as I just loved to be around animals and in fact my first ambition as a child had been to become a vet.

That dream died when I killed my pet duck which I had dosed with human medicine when I thought it had a cold!

That human medicine was white rum mixed with honey and lime, which I had heard worked like a charm. Even now, I often wonder if I had actually interred my poor little ducking alive, for I remember how I had quickly buried it before an adult could see what had happened since it had stiffened immediately after I dosed it.

Suppose it had only been drunk, I often ask myself even now?

As I said before, I had owned and operated two lucrative children's nurseries before moving to the farm, one in Kingston and one in Edgewater in St. Catherine, but I was so taken up with the idea of becoming a great farmer, I immediately sold them both. However, with little money left after making the down-payment, I could not buy the animals needed to make my dream come through. I therefore prepared a business plan to operate a dairy, using the feedstock method instead of open range roaming, as most of the land was already in rice.

I then applied to the government-operated Agricultural Credit Bank (ACB) for a loan and was extremely excited when an officer visited the farm, looked over the facilities and the proposal and assured me they would have no problem financing the project.

Then he dropped the bombshell.

To get the project passed and the loan approved, I would have to give him a kickback of 20% of the principal that I wanted to borrow! (It was revealed many years later when there was an enquiry into the lending policies of that institution, that it was the beleaguered taxpayers who had been saddled with the losses incurred by the lending policies there. For loans had been given out willy-nilly to persons without any form of collateral or just simply to political activists aligned to the ruling party but not even involved in farming.) I can only wonder now whether the non-activists or rather, real farmers, who got loans then, were successful because they had been prepared to pay kickbacks!

We will never know, but as far back as I can remember, some degree of corruption has been, a never-ending burden that the Jamaican taxpayer has regularly been called on to bear, regardless of which party forms the government!

But I stray.

Of course, at the time that kickback was being demanded of me, there was no one to complain to as the majority of persons employed by the government had to be highly accredited party people who gained employment only after meeting the conditions of the "Pickersgillian Accreditation Committee."

That committee was established in the 70's under the chairmanship of Robert Pickersgill, a man who has served on and off, as a Minister in the Jamaican government since the 70's and is dubbed Chairman for life of the PNP.

89

The function of that body was to guarantee the political purity of persons being employed in the government service.

Without the capital that the loan would have provided, I had to bite my lips and settle for limited egg production with around 200 chickens, which was all I could scrounge up enough money to purchase. I really started to enjoy being a farmer for soon I was able to add ducks and other small stock as I went along.

We also planted about 5 acres of coconuts on a section that was not under rice production, as we were determined to use up every bit of land. Further, the Coconut Board gave farmers free coconut plants if one signed an agreement to sell the copra back to them, when the trees started to bear. Copra is the raw material from which coconut oil is manufactured.

On the farm itself, I remember the difficulty we had getting people to plant the coconut suckers though. In fact, we had to get workers from outside the area to do the planting. But would you believe that after we paid people to plant the coconuts, PNP activists came in and pulled up most of the plants, saying they were "capturing" some to plant on their own land! They could have also gotten suckers free of cost but preferred to go around *capturing* other people's things. "Capturing" had quickly become the latest fad which became the fertilizer for the epidemic of *praedial larceny,* which even now, is crippling numerous farmers.

It was also only a matter of time before the entire place was invaded by political sycophants who abused us constantly for being "wicked capitalists." In retrospect therefore, I really should not have been shocked when one morning I woke up to find my chicken house totally empty.

That put paid to my intentions to continue farming as I had no more money to restock anyway. The good thing though was that rice could not be stolen as it could only be reaped mechanically.

At that time rice farming was a big industry throughout the parish of St. Catherine and there was even a rice mill in Spanish Town which supplied 25% of the country's demand.

However, there was only one rice combine in the parish but this effectively reaped all the huge rice plantations all the way down to Hill Run at the southern tip of the parish. But like so many other persons who were fleeing Jamaica, the owner of the reaper decided to move to Belize, taking his equipment with him.

To fill the gap, a government agency, the Agricultural Development Corporation (ADC), bought four rice reapers from Russia to replace the *one* that had done the job before. But would you believe that when you wanted the use of a reaper you could not get one!

For true to form, when government operates anything, there is nothing but massive inefficiency and other problems, including outright corruption.

So those reapers were not properly maintained; there were no spare parts and the workers got involved in the "national past-time" of stealing everything that was not nailed down as the new chant was "socialist time, we own eberyting" (it was socialist time so everything on the island was theirs.) So soon all the reapers were scrapped, thus putting them permanently out of commission.

That was the beginning of the end of rice production in St. Catherine and today I do not think you can find a grain of rice there.

I remember our last crop vividly, for when the rice was ready to be reaped, we could not find a reaper to rent. In desperation, we even tried the impossible.

We sought out laborers from near and far and attempted the frustrating and laborious task of reaping some 30 acres by hand. We had to give up after a day or two however and accept the fact that we had been totally wiped out. For trying to reap that amount of rice by hand would have cost us at least three times more than what we would earn selling the product to the mill!

Jumping Into Politics Head First

At that time living in relatively safe Spanish Town, I was becoming more and more involved in political activity, for despite being terrorized, having his key organizers detained under the State of Emergency and recently losing the 1976 elections, Seaga seemed to have become invigorated and decided to fight back.

I immediately established a local JLP branch to do grassroots organization in my community and started to visit the JLP headquarters at Belmont Road in Kingston, as often as I could, to see how I could help with anything.

Incidentally, at that time, I had a little Suzuki 50 bike which was perfect for getting around on the narrow streets in Spanish Town and which my young kids really loved to ride around on with me on the farm. Besides, with the chronic shortage of petrol, it suited me superbly.

When I took the kids on the regular jaunts on the farm, my late son being older, would sit at the back and my daughter in the front. Even when we all fell and tears flowed, in no time they would be up, pleading to get back on.

While I initially used it for local travel within Spanish town and to have fun with the kids, I eventually started to venture to Kingston, 15 miles away, on my little bike.

At that time, I had never seen another woman riding a bike except one traffic cop who rode a huge one; probably four times the size of mine. One afternoon, as I was returning from Kingston on my little bike, I saw her coming full speed behind me and as the police at the time were totally political and targeted JLP activists and I had already recognized that I was under scrutiny, I figured I was in big trouble.

I say I was being targeted as there was an Inspector Stewart in charge of the capital, Spanish Town in St. Catherine, who made it clear to me that my movements would be monitored and restricted. (In his book "Roots Radical," Jamaican author Errol Stephenson, admitted that he was paid $40.00 per week by the Special Branch arm of the Police Force, to monitor me and report back to them and I have no doubt at all that this was true).

The very first time I saw this Inspector, was at the gate of a manufacturing establishment in Spanish town that we called the "acid factory." It was so named locally because it produced a type of acid used by the bauxite companies in the manufacturing of aluminum.

Incidentally, that factory was owned by a Barclay Ewart who was reputed to be the best friend of the then Prime Minister, Michael Manley. However, Manley had the well-earned reputation of being a lady killer who "rewarded" his friends by sleeping with their wives!

Ewart's ex-wife became Manley's fifth wife sometime after a public scandal about her alleged infidelity with him, had surfaced.

But that's an aside.

Residents living close to that factory faced serious problems because the emissions had been creating an environmental nightmare for them, which even led to some people developing respiratory problems. Further, the toxic acid residue which it expelled into the atmosphere through large chimneys was landing on the zinc roofs of nearby houses, burning huge holes into them, which eventually led to severe leaking in those dwellings.

Shortly after I went to live in Spanish Town, I became aware of the problem and the unresponsiveness of the company to the plight of the suffering citizens. On hearing that they were mounting demonstrations every Monday morning at the factory gate and blocking the entry and exit of everyone who wanted to do business there, I decided to join them regularly, to try and force the company to take remedial action.

The very first time I arrived at the scene, the police were already there but would you believe as I rode up, Stewart loudly declared "yes the troublemaker is here now" and immediately threatened me with arrest and forced us to disperse.

On another occasion, as I was demonstrating in Spanish Town and giving out pamphlets, the same Stewart confiscated my package of anti-government pamphlets and ordered them destroyed!

However, even before Stewart targeted me, I had started to build up a total dislike and distrust for our police, not only because they had become blatantly politicized after the State of Emergency; had been using their awesome powers to lock up and harass non-socialists without cause and were tear gassing us whenever we gathered to demonstrate, but also I had even been recently locked up by one in a most unfair situation.

I had taken my mom to a funeral in the mid-island parish of Clarendon where she was born, and afterward had driven her to my childhood home where she still lived, in St. Elizabeth. Leaving St. Elizabeth for Kingston about 4 am the next morning in an attempt to get to work on time, I had stopped at the only traffic light in the mid-island town of Mandeville, as it was red. However, as crime was escalating and people were being surprised by criminals at traffic lights in Kingston at dark, lonely intersections, I wasn't about to take any chances even in Mandeville. So, when I saw no other cars around at the intersection, I drove off before the light changed to green. I of course hadn't seen the police car parked at the gas station nearby so was really shocked when I heard the siren behind me.

When the cop caught up with me, he was reeking of stale rum and immediately started to verbally abuse me severely, interspersing his diatribe with curse words. Angrily I had told him back a few of the choice bad words he had told me, only to have him react by pulling out his gun, point it at me and drag me off to jail in Mandeville. So really, I had come to expect nothing but harassment and unpleasant interaction with the police.

Since past encounters with the police had made me wary of them, I was pleasantly surprised when the aforementioned female cop drew up beside me and started a conversation by commenting that she had never seen another woman riding a bike before.

After the ice was broken, she rode a couple miles beside me and we chatted about everything and that was when I learnt her name was Ionie Ramsay and she was a Sergeant of police. We remained friends for quite a few years after that though we never ever had a political discussion.

Around that time, the violence had been escalating rapidly and although the "civil war" remained undeclared and even now some people have refused to admit that it happened, Jamaica did have *a fully blown civil war* which lasted from early 1977 to October 30th 1980. It only ceased after the 1980 general election was held.

To prop up their forces the PNP had been sending young men to be trained in guerrilla warfare in Cuba and they were being armed by the Russians and Cubans while the JLP's gunmen were being armed by the American CIA, it was alleged.

I am convinced that had that state of emergency been really used to ferret out the gunmen from both parties, instead of just locking up JLP activists and supporters, Jamaica would never have become the violent nation it has, keeping us for years among the top 5 murder capitals of the world.

Therefore, as the 1976 State of Emergency was ineffective, things went from bad to worse. Our streets became literal battlegrounds and one of the most dangerous corridors in Kingston was the road to the International Airport. For on Mountain View Avenue, the main road to that gateway, there were warring factions living across the road from each other and they seemed to relish firing wildly on the public thoroughfare during peak hours.

In addition, hundreds of persons, aside from those being seriously injured or killed in political battles, were left homeless as the burning of the houses of political rivals became somewhat of a past-time among many activists. I do not think one parish was left unscathed by the violence, pockets of which were everywhere although not all to the extent as it was in the capital city.

Not even the police were safe as there were frequent assaults on their stations. It was the children who were affected most of all though as schools in volatile areas had to be closed frequently. Even if the schools were not closed, absenteeism born of fear, became frequent. Even where children attended the schools, in some areas they were unable to concentrate because of the constant gunfire.

There were also some especially gruesome atrocities being committed, the likes of which had never before been heard of in the English-Speaking Caribbean. The main ones have been widely reported elsewhere and anyone who wishes to be reminded in full of the gory details can find the information easily in the newspaper archives.

What I am doing here is just giving a synopsis of the more outrageous acts.

The ones that will forever stand out in my mind are the *Orange Lane Fire, the Green Bay Massacre, the Gold Street Massacre* and *the Moonex Affair*. The latter, undoubtedly the most troubling, involved the Cubans in apparent complicity with the then Jamaican minister of Security Dudley Thompson, flooding Jamaica with some 200,000 rounds of shotgun cartridges to arm the PNP gunmen and most likely eliminate those who opposed them.

But let's start at the beginning.

On May 19, 1976 ten people were killed in a fire set by gunmen at a tenement building on Orange Lane in a Kingston inner-city. This was a low-cost housing complex and it was burnt to the ground by armed arsonists. So brutal were these terrorists that it was revealed at a later enquiry that they had prevented the residents from getting out of the burning building by firing shots at them as they tried to escape the inferno.

Even babies were not spared as it was also reported that some gunmen even grabbed the infants from their rescuers and threw them back into the burning building.

This was probably the most sickening and horrific crime ever committed in the country as it involved the deliberate burning to death of helpless children.

A year later a commission of enquiry was held into that monstrous event under the chairmanship of a highly respected former Supreme Court Judge Ronald Small, a man whose family had always been politically involved with the ruling PNP. Among his published findings was the confirmation that Manley's minister of housing, Anthony Spaulding, who had always been rumored to be involved in arming gunmen and directing affairs in his garrison located at Arnett Gardens which is close to Orange Lane;

> *"...was a man with more than a blushing acquaintance with gunmen."*

(The full report of the Commission of Enquiry into the Orange Lane fire is well hidden in the Rare Books section of the library at Institute of Jamaica at East Street in Kingston).

However, that was as close as an apparently fearful Small would come to attributing responsibility, for he never said who had been directly responsible for that dastardly act in the dangerously polarized country of ours. (Subsequent leaks by a close family member years later, revealed that Small's entire family had to live with serious threats to their lives during the period when that enquiry was being conducted.)

Although I have to divert a bit, I actually experienced Spaulding's "blushing acquaintance with gunmen."

This happened a few days after the then Cuban Ambassador, Ulysses Estrada went on national television and threatened "....to bring in his soldiers to deal with those of us who were criticizing his government." Some of us were so incensed by this brazen threat in our own country that the JLP drafted a letter to the prime minister demanding that Estrada be immediately expelled from Jamaica. To deliver the letter, quite a few hundred of us marched to the prime minister's office at Jamaica House on Hope Road in Kingston.

However, the security would not allow us to enter the property or even take the letter from us. While we were arguing with him at the gate, up drove a car and we saw Anthony Spaulding sitting in the back. Beside him was a man I did not recognize but immediately saw the gun he raised through the back window and aimed at the crowd.

I later learnt that the shooter had been one of Spaulding's gunmen called "Red Tony" or "Tony Red," I really do not recall exactly.

What I do remember however is that I broke every record that Usain Bolt could only dream of, as on seeing the gun aimed at us, I ran non-stop from Hope Road to Belmont road (JLP headquarters) a distance of around five miles. So frightened was I and being totally propelled by adrenalin, I never even knew that I had lost my shoes somewhere along the road until

I reached my destination and someone asked me what had happened to them? I had no idea where I lost them then and still do not know as I reflect on the matter.

Of course, at the time the police force had been totally politicized with most of senior officers openly working along with Manley's political agenda. So, when we reported the shooting, an Inspector Hewitt came to the JLP headquarters and took statements from all who saw the shooter, but the matter died there.

But back to the massacres.

Next, the Green Bay Massacre was executed by members of the Jamaica Defense Force (JDF) our official army, on January 5, 1978 to assist Michael Manley get better control his constituency.

I have no doubt that Manley himself initiated the entire sordid affair, since the army fell directly under his portfolio and the men killed, were his open and vocal detractors. But as the Manley family was the closest thing we had to royalty in Jamaica, the charismatic Michael did not have much difficulty becoming a "Teflon" politician in the eyes of those who never stopped supporting him, regardless of what he did.

Even his penchant for betraying his best friends by openly seducing their wives and publicly humiliating them, was almost universally accepted as being something to be celebrated by those who worshipped him!

So, it is not unusual that for years, his most ardent propagandists have been either totally successful in convincing, or sowing the seeds of doubt, among a significant number of people. Their line has always been that all the bloody massacres, including the Green Bay Massacre, were not initiated on Manley's orders but instead by the "leftists" who had seized control of the party.

Baloney!

Nothing could be further from the truth for regardless of what appeared to be happening in the public view, Manley had always retained full control of his party.

What led to the Green Bay Massacre was that in his garrison constituency, there was a small JLP enclave called Southside where unemployed young men were demanding that jobs being given out by the government, be distributed equally between JLP and PNP supporters.

This simple demand for justice and fairness was regarded as them not only defying his authority and but also making pests of themselves.

The intelligence division of the army was therefore mandated to single out the "troublesome" fellows, promising them that they would be transported to the army's range at Green Bay to get jobs loading a ship. As pre-arranged, they were picked up by an ambulance belonging to the army. When they arrived at Green Bay, they were instructed to walk ahead of the soldiers. When they reached the pre-determined point, an army sniper hiding in the bushes opened fire on them.

Five of the seven young men were killed on the spot, but fortunately two were able to escape, though seriously hurt.

Of course, the initial information coming out of the from the army had been that they had surprised the men unloading guns from a boat, the men fired on them, the army returned fire and the men were killed.

It was only because one of the two who escaped was able to get to and elicit the assistance of Sister Benedict Chung, a nun who was based and worked in the inner-city, that the true story was leaked to investigative journalists at the Gleaner newspaper and eventually publicized. Photographs found on one of the Officer's camera which showed how the shadows were cast, also substantiated the time the survivors said the incident had occurred. This totally contradicted the army's timeline.

There was a subsequent *show trial,* but the perpetrators got off scot free as the entire thing had been initiated from on high.

The mass murder which I know most about however was the Gold Street Massacre in April 1980. This was when gunmen traveled in canoes from the open sea and fired on a dance in progress at Gold Street, killing several people.

Once again this was in Prime Minister Michael Manley's constituency.

Because of the precision with which that assault had been carried out, killing five persons and injuring more than a dozen, I had always assumed that the Cubans who were visible all over Jamaica at the time, had led that assault. I later learnt, quite by accident, that it was done by our own home-grown boys, some of whom had been trained as "brigadistas" in Cuba.

The first time I ever went to Gold Street which was a JLP enclave in Manley's constituency and coincidentally the same area from which the army had lured the seven young men who they ambushed at Green Bay, was shortly after a newspaper carried a story that JLP supporters had staged a "mock funeral" for Michael Manley and his wife Beverly.

Events such as these were quite common on the Jamaican political scene for decades as many party supporters always relished building elaborate coffins to show that their opponent was "politically" dead. There were never any violent intentions when these mock funerals were staged as it was just a method of political dissention being staged in good fun.

At this point I was working with the JLP full time in their public relations department. This was in the olden days when video cameras were not widely known or used. In fact, the only one I had seen up to then was the huge one carried by the cameramen at the local television station.

However, there was a wealthy Englishman by the name of Phil Harvey who had lived in Jamaica for years. He was a close member of the well-respected family that owned and produced the internationally known brand, Harvey's Bristol Cream Sherry and he later became one of the founders of the Jamaican Film Industry.

Phil owned a video camera and had also been helping out at

the JLP headquarters, also in the public relations department. When he saw the story and pictures of the attractively decorated coffin at mock funeral in the newspaper, he suggested to me that we go downtown and video tape the procession for possible propaganda purposes at a later date.

So off we went to Gold Street, having made contact with someone there who had promised to have the scene we saw in the newspaper, re-enacted. It was quite a jolly affair with everyone being a film star for a day and we the directors. The "stars" enjoyed themselves immensely as they walked somberly with the flower-decorated coffin on their heads, in which were the effigies of Manley and his wife.

They even sang funeral hymns as they ambled along.

Little did we know or expect that retaliation to what was just a little innocent fun would have been the swift, bloody assault on revelers, the very next night at a fundraising dance.

But in retrospect, maybe we should have known that "dissing" (disrespecting) the ultimate leader, not once but twice, would have really angered him and his supporters.

I have never written or spoken about it before, but I have always felt a measure of guilt for possibly having contributed to that retaliation. For if the mock funeral had not been re-enacted, maybe, *just maybe*, the bloodthirsty, vengeful, power hungry ones would not have assaulted the innocent revelers.

Another thing is I had always thought was that raid had been carried out by the Cubans or even under their supervision. For in my book it had been too precise to have been implemented by our then, unsophisticated gangsters. Besides, the terrorists had come in from the sea to carry out the attack and I had never heard of anything like that happening in Jamaica before.

I was only disabused of that impression, many years later.

This happened sometime in the early 80's after I had become quite friendly with a former president of the PNP Youth Organization (PNPYO), Norris MacDonald.

We had both been doing political commentary at the now defunct JBC radio after the change of government. Then all political views were being welcomed by the station in an effort to try and restore their damaged credibility. For during the 70's the government-owned JBC had become what Seaga later described as, a "sewer pit" as the news was always manipulated to become propaganda, not provide information. So, our presence there was after the biased group which had commandeered the station before the 1980 elections, had been fired.

Norris had suggested to me that since we had both been political activists on opposite sides and knew the inner workings of the parties, we should do a political investigative/discussion program for television.

As we looked into the format and the types of interviews we would conduct, one of the places we visited was part of Manley's garrison at Hanover Street in downtown Kingston. There Norris introduced me to a young man whose first name I cannot remember but his surname was Mothersill. Because his name was so uncommon and I was hearing it for the first time, I had enquired where he was from and he told me that he had been born in St. Mary but grew up in Kingston.

He claimed he was the don of the area, so during a very wide and varied conversation, I started slipping in questions to him about the Gold Street massacre, since it had been carried out right there in that garrison constituency.

At one point I suggested to him that I thought it had been carried out by the Cubans; a) because of the precision of the attack and b) the fact that the attackers had come from the sea, something unprecedented in Jamaica.

His answer was immediate, boastful and terse; "No a wi dweet," (No we did it) he said. When he realized what he had inadvertently revealed, he refused to continue but did admit that the police had detained and questioned him about it but they had no evidence to hold him or anyone else. I had to cease asking anything further about it as his quick change of attitude made me realize that I was treading in dangerous waters.

An Act of Treason

The implications of the Moonex Affair were the most far-reaching for Jamaica as a sovereign nation and even raised the real possibility that our then minister of security Dudley Thompson had been involved in *treason*.

On the 7th May, 1980, an innocent looking consignment on a boat arriving in Jamaica was being inspected by Customs officers when to their shock; they discovered that the cargo was 19,000 pounds of cartridges for sawn- off shotguns. This shipment was destined for a firm in Kingston named Moonex International, the manager of which was one Ruperto Hart.

I cannot recall how the stories started or were reported, but soon it came out that Moonex was a Cuban-owned company and they were trying to smuggle in the bullets under diplomatic cover.

At first, the then Cuban Ambassador and apparent DGI boss, Ulysses Estrada vehemently denied that Moonex had anything to do with Cuba. He quickly got the willing assistance of persons in the JBC newsroom in his attempt to do damage control. (It was not only that media house where the news was being manipulated though, for at that time the Press Association of Jamaica (PAJ) had also been taken over by PNP/communist activists who made it their business to distort the news in every media house they worked.) However, the process was more concentrated at JBC than elsewhere.

During the 70's, some of the better-known activists working in the JBC newsroom were; Hopeton Dunn, (now a professor at the University of the West Indies (UWI) and former head of the Broadcasting Commission in Jamaica); Brian Meeks, (currently a professor at a US university); Colin Campbell, still an active member of the PNP in which he once served as General Secretary and later became a minister in the government. In 2006 he resigned after becoming entangled in an international bribery scandal dubbed the "Trafigura affair" involving our government and a Dutch company named Trafigura; (That matter is still before the courts); Anthony Bogues, (now a professor at Brown University in the USA);

the late John Maxwell, who was for years a journalist but was always an overt and active PNP politician at the same time.

That newsroom had by then been almost totally discredited by well thinking persons because they had gained such notoriety for manipulating the news. In fact, the news report that stands out most graphically in my mind up to today was the amazing report which convinced even PNP supporters that what was emanating from that institution was unadulterated propaganda and not news.

This was their coverage of a robbery in Half Way Tree in Kingston.

For the benefit of those who do not know much about the geography of Kingston, Half Way Tree Road is the major thoroughfare that runs from downtown to uptown Kingston, although there may be name changes along the away. Half Way Tree itself is also considered midtown the capital city of Kingston. (The parishes of Kingston and St. Andrew were merged in 1923. Before that, Kingston's northern boundary was Half Way Tree Square.)

The robbery had been carried out in the middle of that commercial area close to where JBC was located. However, the news report that came from that station and which appalled listeners stated that;

> "............the robbers made their escape by jumping into a car and making their way down Half Way Tree road in the direction of the JLP stronghold of Tivoli Gardens...."

Even now, rereading this ridiculous news item in a column I had written for a newspaper at the time, causes me to laugh uncontrollably.

You see, Tivoli Gardens lies quite a few miles to the west of Half Way Tree Road. So, persons driving down that road could have been far more likely be heading to other garrison areas such as nearby Kencot, Slipe Pen Road, Arnett Gardens or Fletchers Land.

Broadcasting therefore that the vehicle was heading towards Tivoli Gardens was probably the most graphic display of the type of news distortion that had become the norm at the radio station. It was because of the reputation those "journalists" there had earned for themselves by producing *fake news*, why Seaga was widely applauded when he referred to that government owned and operated organization as a "Sewer Pit" and almost as a first act, fired the entire newsroom when he gained power in 1980.

But back to the Moonex Affair.

On May 11th 1980, in an article entitled "Desperate Times" well-known Gleaner columnist Wilmot Perkins wrote;

> *"The J. B. C. panicked. It couldn't endure the nervous strain of such a thing just hanging loose.' It had to be pinned, and pinned quickly, and pinned to the Opposition. The J. B. C did its duty to the revolution. It declared to its listeners that Ruperto Hart, Manager of Moonex International Establishment, the illegally-operating company that had illegally imported the ammunition into Jamaica,*

was a blood Relative of a prominent J.L.P. supporter of the same name. It thus invited the inference that it was the J L.P. that was bringing ammunition into Jamaica to supply political gunmen. Significantly, he Minister of tNational Security, makes similar innuendo in relation to other members and supporters of the J.L.P. in the statement issued to the news media on Friday. But measures attempted in panic are seldom sustainable, and this was no exception. Ruperto Hart is not related to the J.LP's Hart; nor indeed is he related to the PNP"s Hart. The J.B.C. had to 'retreat in a flurry of apologies, leaving behind an impression that something sinister was afoot which it had tried and failed to pin on the J.L.P therefore inviting the question, if not the J.L.P. who?"

"The behavior of the Minister of National Security, Mr. Thompson, has been. to say the least, peculiar. His stance is not that of the investigator. Still less is it that of leader of the hounds," as was the case in the affair of the American Embassy 'cameras'. Mr. Thompson this time is stoutly defending, not the security interests of Jamaica, but Moonex and the Cuban Embassy, and Cuba itself. This affair of the shot-gun cartridges and Mr. Thompson's handling of it can only heighten that fear. For defend as he might, the Cuban connection remains clear. The strain of the Government is too great. It cannot make Mr. Ruperto Hart into a Jamaican. This is curious as Mr. Estrada, the Cuban Ambassador, admitted to me on Friday that Hart is Cuban."

Mr. Perkins then concluded,

"The country has powerful reasons for apprehending a threat of violence from the direction of Cuba, in support of the Government and Party that Mr. Thompson represents. This affair of the shot-gun cartridges and Mr. Thompson's handling of it can only heighten that fear. For defend as he might, the Cuban connection remains clear."

Then in an article in the Venezuelan magazine *Zeta* in June 1980, commenting on the Moonex affair, it was revealed that;

"Moonex is one of the many companies which is used by Castro's people to introduce their agents and spies into other countries. All of them, like Moonex, are in the absolute ownership of the Cuban dictatorship and their executives are selected by the Intelligence Service."

The full extent of Thompson's treachery was revealed in an investigative report in the Gleaner dated June 19, 1980 entitled; "Moonex man barred from flying to Cuba, was in a plane with Thompson, Estrada." It stated;

"Moonex International establishment manager Ruperto Hart was yesterday prevented by Immigration officials at the Norman Manley Airport from going on a flight to Cuba on which other passengers were National Security Minister Dudley Thompson and Cuban Ambassador Ulises Estrada.

Hart, whose company had illegally imported shotgun cartridges had arrived here from Miami in a consignment without an import license, is on an Immigration Department "Watch List". A "stop order" preventing him from travelling out of the island is in force. Estrada also accompanied him."

It continued;

"Mr. Thompson made the trip alone, as Mr. Estrada elected to remain behind with Mr. Hart after the Immigration authorities prevented Mr. Hart from leaving. Reports reaching the GLEANER are that yesterday afternoon the travel documents of Thompson, Estrada and Hart were processed by Immigration at Norman Manley International airport for a flight to Cuba. Their baggage was loaded on a Cubana flight; but they boarded a smaller plane. By this time Immigration officials found that Hart was on their "Watch List" and went to the small aircraft they learned he had boarded.

Mr. Hart had been warned for prosecution under two sections of the Customs Act in connection with a consignment of shotgun cartridges which arrived at Bustamante Port on May 5, The GLEANER understands that further legal action was to be taken against him this week. On the plane when the Immigration officials boarded it the Gleaner understands. Mr. Thompson was sitting at the back with his face covered by a paper. Immigration authorities said they were told that Hart was "A Ministry official".

"A Ministry official!"

Can you believe the level of treachery that the Minister of "Security" of Jamaica was involved in, with the full consent of Manley himself, I have no doubt!

Of course, some persons may be wondering how so many people in the "system," were in such dangerous times, not only leaking so much information about what was happening but also enforcing the law against powerful government officials.

It was however this type of cooperation by patriotic persons in the "system" who decided that death was better than dishonor, which greatly assisted in helping to save the country and its citizens from losing their freedoms. For when patriotic persons in numerous government agencies who had previously supported Manley, realized what he was really up to, they became so opposed to Jamaica being brought under Cuban domination resulting in their total loss of freedoms, that they started leaking information to the media and the JLP on a regular basis.

This gave the opposition constant ammunition to allow them to come out vociferously and militantly against the direction in which the government was leading the country, mobilize patriotic Jamaicans to swell their ranks and gain solidarity with international organizations such as Amnesty International and the International Press Association (IAPA.)

Remember too, at that time, the cold war was raging and Manley was attracted by the grandeur of supreme power that Castro had in Cuba. He however also wanted to be regarded by the outside world as a "democrat" when he attended such organizations as the United Nations and Non-Aligned Movement. So, he was always trying to do a balancing act.

With the foreign press keeping an eagle eye on developments here, that also gave the opposition good wiggle room and prevented the Manley regime from taking too many more retaliatory, oppressive and overt actions against those fighting to preserve democracy, although they did get away with locking up a number of JLP leaders and supporters without charge, under the State of Emergency.

Further, as Michael Manley who loved being adored and idolized, started to sense the mounting dislike and loss of personal and party support locally because of the unpopular and often brutal socialist policies, he waffled regularly, even frequently giving in to the JLP's militant demands that enquiries be held into various atrocities.

The enquiries held were however all for show as no one was ever brought to justice for any of the acts of treason and terrorism committed against innocent civilians by state employees, like the army at Green Bay.

Anyway, so serious had been the implications of the Moonex affair that even the Jamaica Council of Churches (JCC) had to speak out against Thompson. I say *even* as that umbrella organization represented most of the churches at that time but had been captured by so- called "liberation theologists" who actively promoted the socialist thrust, so had been branded by the opposition as "the PNP at prayer."

Even they however did not seem able or willing to condone treason, for they joined other organizations which put a statement out on radio, calling on the prime minister to revoke Dudley Thompson's appointment as Minister of Security.

Amazingly though, when Thompson died in 2012, he was actually awarded a State funeral, fully paid for by the Jamaican taxpayer whom he had sought to betray!

Anyway, at that time, not everyone in Manley's cabinet was prepared to sell out Jamaica's interest to the Cubans, for Ministers David Coore, Eric Bell and Vivian Blake all resigned from the cabinet although they said nothing to the Jamaican people about why they were leaving.

On the other hand, a junior minister named Allan Isaacs not only resigned but crossed the floor and joined the JLP in the fight to turn back his former colleagues who were dead set on making Jamaica the second communist satellite in the Caribbean. He contested the election for the JLP in Saint Andrew South Eastern in the 1980 elections and won the seat.

As the undeclared civil war raged at the local level, almost every constituency in Jamaica saw some form of violence coming from either the JLP, the PNP or the Trevor Munroe led WPJ which supported the PNP. By the end of 1980, murders had doubled to almost 900 from 440 the previous year for there was no shortage of weapons or ammunition on either side. In fact, I can't recall going to bed any night without hearing numerous gunshots being fired whether nearby in the Grants Pen area or afar.

Of course, travelling around, one had to know which areas to avoid, for in some zones, just being an outsider could lead to your death.

While it was mainly the poor in the garrisons and foot soldiers who were chiefly in the line on fire, at the executive level, during the 1976 election campaign, JLP MP Mike Henry was been shot in York Town, Clarendon but survived. In 1980 former prime Minister Hugh Lawson Shearer was shot in his head with a spear gun by PNP terrorists as he travelled through the town of Falmouth in the northern parish of Trelawny, but he also survived, but the body count constantly escalated among the "masses".

The only high level politician who was actually killed during that period was a parliamentary secretary in the Ministry of Security, Roy McGann.

He was killed in a shootout with police the night before Nomination Day for the 1980 election.

Naturally the police would never have knowingly fired on a group including a government parliamentarian, but they never knew he was there. They had gotten a report that gunmen were firing at JLP supporters in the Gordon Town area of rural St. Andrew, confronted the miscreants and when the smoke had cleared, it was discovered that McGann himself and his police bodyguard had been among the attackers.

That led to a serious reprisal against JLP supporters in the Gordon Town area. Many were beaten, others burnt out of their homes and otherwise terrorized for days as the politically-aligned members of the security forces invaded the area with blood in their eyes and revenge in their hearts.

At that time, Tivoli Gardens and Rema, both in Kingston, were the supreme garrison strongholds of the Jamaica Labour Party, and although regularly and terribly outnumbered by PNP gunmen from the constituencies of Kingston East and Port Royal, Kingston West Central, Kingston East Central, St. Andrew West Central, St. Andrew East Central, St. Andrew Southern, St. Andrew South Western, St. Andrew Western and St. Andrew South Eastern, they remained *invincible* and undaunted so their small territories became impenetrable.

This gave Tivoli Gardens the reputation of being the "Mother of all garrisons" and it retained that reputation up to recently when after the incursion in 2010 by the police/army to arrest their sitting don "Dudus", the constituency was allegedly finally freed from the stranglehold of a "supreme don."

But back to the events of the 70's.

Although by 1978 I had been working at the JLP headquarters almost full time, I had never been to Tivoli Gardens but had certainly heard about some of the fearsome gunmen there.

At the time the supreme don there was Claudius Massop about whom I often heard chilling stories. Among the ones that

118

remain etched in my memory are tales of him outshooting policemen who outnumbered him by up to five to one, and he chasing his girlfriend into the Denham Town police station and parting her hair with a bullet, right in front of the police who dared not arrest him for he was a notoriously ruthless killer, at least by reputation.

He had however gotten some good press for he, along with an arch-rival, the PNP's super don Bucky Marshall, had been instrumental in organizing a peace initiative to try and stop the foot soldiers from both parties, murdering each other as their political leaders had apparently ordered.

This initiative blossomed into the famous "One Love Peace Concert" which featured not only the late superstar Bob Marley and the Wailers but also a host of other reggae and international artists.

It was held at the National Stadium in Kingston on the 22nd April 1978. Some 80,000 fans attended as it was Marley's first performance at home after he had fled into self-imposed exile in England, after an attempt had been made on his life in Jamaica two years earlier. (It was alleged at the time that the attempt on Marley's life had been made because he had agreed to participate in a concert dubbed "Smile Jamaica," which was held in December 1976, just prior to the general election. It was therefore labeled as a political event being used by the government to appease the "masses.")

Massop and Marshall who were street fighters for the two parties, had met while in jail earlier and decided that too many poor people were dying so they should call a truce.

119

They both traveled to England to convince Marley to return to headline the concert and he did.

Also performing was the iconic Mick Jagger of the Rolling Stones. That concert was at the time rated among the top 10 rock concerts in the world by the BBC and called the Third World Woodstock by another media house.

The valuable role played by the former rival dons, (Massop and Marshall) to seek peace and put an end to the bloodshed, was publicly recognized during the concert when they were both called up on stage by Marley, in a symbolic gesture. Marley also called the political leaders, Manley and Seaga to mount the stage to shake hands.

Despite the best efforts of Marley, Massop and Marshall, the divide between the JLP and PNP politicians at the top was so bitter, that they frustrated the efforts of their senior gunmen at the grassroots level, to bring about lasting peace among their supporters and Marshall was murdered shortly after the concert.

I met Massop only by chance. I was at the JLP headquarters at Belmont Road one afternoon and had been having quite an animated conversation with a slightly built, good looking young man. We discussed everything from what was happening in politics locally to international affairs. After about half an hour of interesting conversation, he left and I asked someone in the yard who he was. When I heard that he was the notorious "Claudie Massop, I nearly had a heart attack.

This was because of the stories I had heard about him, but he certainly did not fit the profile I had in my head of what a fierce gunman looked like. In fact, it was more than an image in my head, for I had once encountered one "Early Bird," a PNP gunman some time before and he really looked just as I imagined a gunman should!

At the time I saw Early Bird, I had been very active in a new JLP youth organization called the Nationalist Patriotic Movement (NPM) which had been established under the mentorship of veteran politician and deputy leader of the party, Pernell Charles.

We were young, unafraid, loved street politics like painting graffiti and would demonstrate at the drop of a pin.

Our most successful demonstration was the infamous Gas Demonstration of 1979 which caused the entire country to be locked down by roadblocks for three days.

Incidentally it was Michael Manley himself who first taught Jamaicans how to block roads as he used that method most effectively, I hear, in a strike some years before at JBC, when he was a labor leader in search of political fame. I say I hear, as I had not yet returned home when that strike took place.

That 1979 gas demonstration had the most long-lasting effect on me personally though, as it led to me being detained at Cross Roads police station and facing a possible mandatory prison term of "indefinite detention" for having spent shells.

I say long lasting effect, for when I was locked up, I was given a cigarette to calm my nerves and that led me to take up back and continue with a vice I had discarded some three years before.

The mandatory indefinite detention sentence referred to above was legislated in 1974, when two friends of Prime Minister Manley were shot and killed in close succession. That led him to establish an institution called the "Gun Court" where, under the accompanying legislation, anyone found with even *one* spent shell, would face a mandatory indefinite detention sentence. While the "mandatory" and "indefinite" components were later struck down by the United Kingdom Privy Council as being unconstitutional, during the late 70's it hung over the heads of all and sundry like the sword of Damocles.

Anyway, I was detained because I had a handful of spent shells. I had them, as having been at the JLP headquarters one day, we got word that some peaceful demonstrators who were marching from downtown Kingston to the headquarters, had been fired on by police and soldiers. We decided to march to the spot where we heard the assault by the security forces on peaceful marchers had taken place, to assist the injured and show solidarity to their cause.

On arriving at Old Hope Road in the vicinity of the Regal theatre which is just above Cross Roads which is halfway between Half Way Tree and downtown Kingston, we met upon a few people walking slowly, who had been in the demonstration. They were the ones who had not fled home or been injured when the barrage of shots had been fired into the crowd by the police.

They took us to a spot and pointed to a number of spent M16 automatic rifle shells lying on the ground. These were the shells left behind when the police fired into the group demonstrating. I immediately took up a handful, hoping to present them to the appropriate authorities as evidence of police brutality against peaceful demonstrators.

As we walked towards the nearest police station, led by senior members of the party, I felt something hard and cold being thrust in my back. When I turned around, I realized that it was a long machine gun being held by a soldier who shouted that he was going to have me locked up for having "dangerous weapons." (ie. The spent shells.)

I was scared out of my wits for to begin with, I am terribly claustrophobic. Further, as I walked along in front of him, I had visions of him tripping and the gun going off and blowing a big hole in my back.

Anyway, even if I didn't get killed, there was the specter of my being locked up indefinitely in a nasty Jamaican jail. For the stinking conditions under which prisoners were being held, were no secret. In fact, this had even attracted much condemnation from Amnesty International, for which I had been a local correspondent at that time.

I was taken to the police station at Cross Roads and told to sit on a bench with other prisoners who were waiting to be processed.

Incidentally, sitting right beside me, was a youngster who immediately called me by name. When I asked where he

knew me from, he said he knew the Williams family and had
been reported to the police by my late father-in-law, a
developer, with whom he said he worked. He had been
arrested for allegedly stealing building materials, but he was
not guilty, he confided. He pleaded with me to assist him but I
had to point out to him that I could not even help myself as I
was a prisoner too!

I was a nervous wreck as I was kept waiting on the bench for
about four hours without any attempt being made to lay
charges against me. Every time I enquired about my fate, I
was told that the arresting officer was not around so I would
just have to sit there and keep myself quiet.

I sat quietly for another few hours, getting hungrier by the
minute then saw a policeman who I knew.

When he enquired what I was doing there, I told him of the
trumped-up charges and complained that I was hungry,
wanted my lunch or even some water as the place was hot and
crowded. He told me that lunch had already been served but
as I was not yet officially in custody, I was not entitled to
have any food anyway.

He assured me that I would not like prisoners" lunch however
as it was just boiled rice. It sounded *yucky* but I told him that
the way my tummy was feeling, I would gladly have downed
even *tasteless* boiled rice.

He left and about half an hour later, returned with a small
brown paper bag and give me a cold Guinness and a cigarette
which he said he had bought with his own funds. I thanked

him profusely and although I did not like stout, that one tasted wonderful as did the cigarette.

Hence my taking up the smoking vice again.

Some more time passed slowly by, then I saw Abe Dabdoud, an attorney from the JLP whom I knew, walking into the guard room. He asked me the details of my detention. He then went to see the senior officer in charge of the station to advise him that I was being illegally detained as all I had done was pick up spent shells as evidence of police brutality.

However, as usual, the police were a law unto themselves, having been given supreme power under the State of Emergency. So, he was informed that I would have to be charged and go to court. No dismissal. No bail.

I guess in my desperation I must have fallen asleep, since I am notorious for sleeping anywhere any time. I really don't know how much time elapsed before I was awakened by a boisterous commotion outside the holding area, caused by a loud booming voice asking for me by name.

That most welcome voice was that of a well-known Queens Council (QC) Winston Spaulding who was then a deputy leader of the JLP and later became the Minister of Security when the JLP took office.

Spaulding was also the younger brother of Anthony Spaulding the PNP minister who had become so notorious that he had been described as a man with more than a "passing acquaintance with gunmen."

125

Winston too had been a PNP member but in an interview with the Jamaica Observer in 2002, he candidly declared;

> *"I grew up in a PNP household but after the state of emergency, and the passing of 1974 Gun Court law, I had a problem with the significant human rights abuses of the time, it was a question of conscience. My father also had a change of position as well, and supports the JLP."*

Incidentally, the father to whom he referred was Frank Spaulding who was a long time PNP supporter and had served as Mayor of Kingston and St. Andrew for three terms, under their umbrella.

Spaulding upbraided the officer in charge for detaining me illegally and it took him only about fifteen minutes to get me out of there. His legal arguments were appropriately backed up by some strong, colorful and effective Jamaican curse words and that strategy worked like a charm. I remain eternally grateful to him for that, for the couple hours I had spent without my freedom of movement made me appreciate even more, how important freedom is to me.

Apart from getting involved in demonstrations and other forms of street activity, we the NPM members were prepared to confront the PNP/WPJ/Cubans on any matter. So, on one occasion when our parent party (the JLP) refused to participate in further debates which were being organized by another government propaganda arm, the Jamaica Information Service, (JIS), we decided that we would take them on anyway.

126

The JLP's boycott of those events was justified anyway as these regular fora were being staged island-wide, not to bring information to the electorate, but simply to shore up the PNP's popularity. For the JIS was using taxpayer's money to transport large number of socialists/communist supporters to the venues to harass and intimidate opposition participants.

Further, the panels were terribly skewed with the JIS, PNP and WPJ spokespersons reciting the same line and shouting down the sole opposition spokesperson whenever he or she spoke.

I clearly remember the debate I was sent to participate in on behalf of the NPM, like it was yesterday.

This was a debate on the economy which was rapidly slipping into the doldrums and driving citizens to the edge of penury at the time, due to Manley's socialist policies. The debate was being held in the Garveymeade Community Centre in Portmore in the parish of St. Catherine.

Knowing from my previous sojourn with them how the PNP operated at functions such as these, I went to a nearby JLP stronghold called Naggo Head, St. Catherine to recruit party supporters to come out to cheer for me at the debate. I told them up front that only very vocal persons should come! I even paid for the two buses to transport them, out of my own pocket.

My straightforward instructions to them were;

"Cheer loudly whenever I speak and boo and hiss loudly when PNP, JIS or WPJ representatives open their mouths!"

In addition, I had carried along a number of packages containing pamphlets criticizing the government. As we were in a tough International Monetary Fund (IMF) agreement which caused us to have to undergo severe restrictions, we had used the IMF"s initials to put all economic difficulties conveniently under the label "Is Manley Fault*"* for propaganda purposes. Most effective it was too!

I gave the propaganda leaflets to my supporters immediately as they boarded the buses, instructing that they hand them out to everyone at the venue as soon as they arrived. On arrival, I went inside to where the debate was to be held.

Everyone had been vociferous and eager as we travelled to the venue but shortly after I sat down, I heard loud noises and shouting coming from outside. We all ran out to see what caused the disturbance only to see all my supporters scrambling wildly to get into the buses which were already revving loudly. When the drivers figured everyone had boarded, they took off at top speed into the night with a loud roar.

I subsequently learnt that as my supporters gave out the pamphlets, the well-known PNP gunman from Matthews Lane nicknamed Early Bird, had taken away some and used his lighter to burn them up right in front of my scared supporters. He then demanded that all other persons with pamphlets bring them and throw them at his feet, *or else.*

I had never heard of Early Bird before but some of my supporters knew of his reputation as a vicious killer and when I got close enough to get a good look at him, he certainly did fit the bill. Yes, Early Bird did look like what I had imagined a bloodthirsty hoodlum would look like, really fearsome with scars on his face and all.

However, there I was abandoned by my "cheering crowd" and left totally alone, I thought. I was too proud and stubborn to slink off into the night however, although that is what my instincts were telling me to do. However, I decided to go back inside and make the best of a bad situation.

Luckily for me, a very tall, strong young man named Magnus Williams had stayed behind with me, but I did not know that until later. Magnus was a friend of mine who lived beside our farm at Duncan's Pen in Spanish Town. He was a courageous political activist who was at the time the councilor caretaker for the Duncan's Pen division. He had not travelled in the bus to the debate with my "paid cheering crowd" but had driven over by himself.

When he saw my dilemma, he came up to the platform and insisted that I should not participate in the debate. I was however determined not be intimidated by a bunch of socialists (that's what we called PNP supporters) and told him so.

When the debate began however it was a different ballgame, for every-time I opened my mouth, my words were drowned out by loud boos and hisses coming from the audience. In fact, I don't think I completed one entire sentence that night for they were using the very strategy I had hoped to use on them when I had collected the two busloads of supporters. But my "defenders" had abandoned me and it had come back to haunt me!

Then I saw Magnus once again approaching the platform. Without saying a word, he picked me up, threw me over his shoulder and carried me out of the room to the sound of loud *boos and hisses.*

I don't know if that night I was more frightened by the fearsome sight of Early Bird or the taunts of the loud hostile crowd, but that event demonstrated to us clearly why the senior politicians in the JLP had been avoiding those debates organized by the JIS. So, from that night we too boycotted them!

But I stray, for the point I was making was about what I imagined a gunman looked like. (Like Early Bird!)

Massop looked nothing like that however, for he was good looking, smooth and well-spoken. He was assassinated by the police on 1979 in what was reported to be shootout.

That story however turned out to be a lie because the coroner's report showed that the bullets that they had sprayed him with had all made their mark under his arm. This meant his hands were above his head, ie. he had surrendered, when he was killed. Stories abounded too that after the police killed him, they drove around the Ministry of Security building downtown several times, firing celebratory shots.

The notorious Dudley Thompson was the Minister of Security at the time.

According to subsequent eyewitness reports given at the Coroner's Inquest, Massop had been returning from a football match in Spanish Town in a taxi, along with friends Lloyd Fraser and Trevor Tinson. The taxi driver gave evidence that the men were unarmed and the inquest found that Massop was shot forty times, mostly under his arm. Because the coroner's report said clearly that it was not a shootout as the police had claimed but murder, some policemen were arrested and there was a trial, but as is usual with those show trials, no one was found culpable.

His murder became symbolic of the excesses the *political police* were using against opposition activists at all levels. At his funeral which was held in West Kingston, some 15,000 of us marched, protesting his murder and government oppression in general.

That was the first time I ever visited Tivoli Gardens and I certainly enthusiastically participated in that march which was disrupted often by the police firing shots into the air and turning us back by teargassing us at regular intervals.

Anyway, during the civil war it was clear that JLP gunmen were as well armed as the PNP's. When I decided to start working a division in Naggo Head with a view to running for the parish council seat in St. Catherine Parish Council, each time I visited a branch meeting, the first thing the young men asked me for was guns.

When I insisted that I had no guns, they told me that there were plenty at "headquarters" (meaning JLP headquarters at Belmont Road) and I should ask for some. I was never interested in getting involved in that aspect of politics however and although I was at the headquarters almost every day for about two years, I never heard of a strong room, an arm's room or any such area at the headquarters.

Neither did I ever ask anyone if I could get arms or from where.

But guns were everywhere in the society and one had to be ultra-careful. I recall one day driving to the JBC radio station at Odeon Avenue in Half Way Tree from Belmont Road, to take in a news release. (Remember in those days there were no smart phones or emails, so hard copies of news releases had to be taken in manually). As I waited for the traffic light to change to green at Knutsford Blvd and Barbados Avenue in New Kingston, I heard a bullet *zing* past my right ear. I had no idea where it was coming from but I never stopped at a traffic light again for that entire day!

I vividly remember too, the graphic reports of the incident that took place on the day when Tom Tavares-Finson was trying to become nominated as the candidate for the JLP in 1980 general election in the St. Andrew South constituency. He was running against Portia Simpson-Miller who later became Jamaica's first female Prime Minister. This was a well-armed garrison that the former minister Anthony Spaulding had established for his protégé Simpson-Miller.

That day Tavares-Finson had to be transported to the nomination center in *an army tank* as every time he and his supporters tried to drive in a section of Spanish Town Road that passed through the constituency, (Spanish Town Road is the main corridor that runs between downtown Kingston and Spanish Town) his party was turned back because they came under heavy gunfire. As bad as things were, I had never heard of another incident anywhere else in the entire island where a candidate had to be escorted by an army tank to a nomination center.

I suspect however that the army was only brought in to protect that opposition candidate for those elections, as by then, the country was swarming with members of the foreign press and lots of outside "election observers," most of whom were concentrated in the capital city. For Michael Manley who saw himself as a leader of the "third world," was very conscious of his *international* reputation so he did everything, including allowing in foreign observer missions for those elections, to try and convince the outside world that he was not really an undemocratic despot schooled by Cuban handlers, despite the evidence to the contrary on the ground.

As the guns continued barking everywhere, I recall one night visiting a "branch" meeting in a really dark, remote and depressed section of Naggo Head. To get there I had to park my car and walk up a dirt-covered foot-path for a couple hundred yards.

After the meeting, an old man who reeked of rum, approached me and told me that as it was dark and possibly dangerous, I should not be walking back to the car by myself, so he was going to accompany me to protect me. He looked so old, shaky and clearly drunk that I decided to humor him. When I reached the car however, opened the door and the light came on, I saw that he was holding a gun in his hand! All I could think of on the way home was how lucky I had been that he had not stumbled in his drunken state and accidentally shot me!

There was also this amusing incident with another so-called "protector." I had been driving over to Naggo Head alone a couple times per week to campaign, when a young man whom I had always seen hanging around the headquarters asked if I did not want him to travel with me in case the car broke down or I had any other problems.

I thought it was a good idea as I sometimes came back quite late and travelled alone, so I told him fine. The next evening as we headed down Hagley Park Road and came to the intersection at Waltham Park Road, I stopped at the red light there. As we waited for the light to change, I saw him take a fast dive under the dashboard of the car. Shocked, I asked him what he was doing and heard a quivering voice coming from below saying "Police." I looked across the road and did see a police car parked there with the lights flashing but I did not understand the reason for his reaction.

When the light changed and I drove off, he gingerly raised himself slowly from under the dashboard. I immediately enquired why he had been hiding from the police. I was absolutely shocked when he told me brazenly that he was wanted by the police for housebreaking. Stupidly, I asked him why the hell he was breaking into peoples' homes only to have him reply, "Is all right Miss Will, is only PNP people house I man bruk." (I only break into homes belonging to PNP supporters!)

As soon as we had driven a safe distance away, I told him to get out of my car and needless to say, I never took him with me again. In retrospect, I can't but be amazed at how naïve and trusting I was in those days, assuming that all who said they were fighting to preserve our freedoms were decent, law abiding, honorable people!

The war continued everywhere on the island to different degrees, but it was especially fierce at the street level, in Kingston and Spanish Town. Not even school children were spared because if they were seen wearing the "wrong color uniform," they became targets.

In those days, the official color of the JLP was green, the PNP orange and the WPJ red. Now neither the poor kids nor their parents had much control over the color of their school uniforms, neither could the people who chose them ever imagine that a day would come in Jamaica when the color of a school uniform could be considered politically offensive.

But it did and if kids who had to pass through or lived in hostile areas were seen in the "wrong" colors, they were often ordered to take off the displeasing color; their parents had to send them to school in ordinary nonoffending clothes or simply keep them home.

During that period, children lost hundreds of valuable school hours because of violence or the threats of violence, but of course the children of the political elite were not affected as

135

they certainly did not live in the worse affected areas. (ie. ghettos!)

While the dangerous intimidation of students wearing the "wrong colors" was pervasive in the capital city and Spanish Town, I was absolutely amazed when it was reported in a newscast that the administration of the Manchester High School in the mid-island town of Mandeville, had closed that institution for more than a week because of the threats to the lives of its students wearing their green uniforms. This was an especially distressing report as it was coming out of what was always considered a peaceful rural community. Had the news come out about a school in a garrison area, it would not have made the news or even caused an eyebrow to be raised at that time, so polarized had we become.

While the violence continued unabated, Manley tried to take aim at the free press which Jamaica had always enjoyed, by demanding that the Gleaner, the most influential medium in the country, send its investigative articles and columns to parliament for approval before publication!

It was only the courage of outstanding columnists such as *Wilmot Perkins, John Hearne, David Dacosta* and Gleaner Editor, *Hector Wynter*, who put their lives on the line and endangered their own freedoms by refusing to comply, why we have the press freedom we continue to enjoy today.

When the Gleaner started to run low on funds, it issued a debenture and the Jamaican public put their money where their mouths were and over-subscribed to it. For after Manley accompanied by the Cuban ambassador Ulysses Estrada, had led a march of rowdy, threatening activists and supporters to the newspaper to intimidate the reporters and columnists, this really incensed the nervous public.

It was a grateful Oliver Clarke, former chairman and managing director of the Gleaner who reminisced in 2000 at that newspaper's 165th anniversary celebration saying;

> *"In the middle 1970's, the Gleaner was a major advocate of private enterprise and democracy in Jamaica. As a result, it came into fairly sharp conflict with the Michael Manley-led government of the time. The company was in fairly bad financial condition. The stock market was in the doldrums. So in 1978 we put out a debenture issue for the grand sum of four million Jamaican dollars. At the time it was the biggest public offering in the history of Jamaica.*
>
> *People rallied around; it was oversubscribed. Even more than the money was the strong vote of confidence demonstrated by the public for the Gleaner. Many major businesses supported the debenture, as well as many hundreds of individuals. This success allowed The Gleaner to pay off its major debts and widen its shareholder base. The debenture issue gave the company a whole new breath of life."*

That debenture, I may add, was critical to the Gleaner being able to import newsprint to continue publishing, as after Michael Manley had led his infamous mob there and threated them with "next time," (meaning next time the staff would not get off so easy!) it was moot as to whether he would

137

follow the example of his fellow anti- press-freedom colleague the late Forbes Burnham then prime minister of Guyana. Burnham had used the claim of shortage of foreign exchange to starve the Starboek News and other newspapers in his country, of newsprint because they criticized his regime. So it was not untoward that there was constant fear in Jamaica that the same strategy would be used, as Burnham and Manley saw themselves as revolutionaries walking hand in hand to the mountain top with Fidel Castro.

In any event, claiming that because the country was suffering from a shortage of foreign exchange, they would have to cut down on the importation of newsprint, would have found some favor with a significant number of persons, especially in light of the shortage of basic foods which was a direct result of the drop in foreign currency earnings.

What I suspect prevented Manley from taking that route is that unlike Burnham, he was very concerned about what people in the outside world thought of him. So, with the foreign press reporting to the world just about everything that was happening in Jamaica at the time, he tried his best to show them a different side of his government, so restricting paper to the press was not a chance he was prepared to take.

This is also why he even allowed commissions of enquiry to be held into the terrible massacres that his party was perpetrating against the Jamaican people, as the opposition JLP was always vociferously calling for these, and the public and the international community were supportive of these calls. I reiterate though that none of the perpetrators of any of the massacres was ever convicted of anything, regardless of what the enquiries found! And recommendations made in those reports were quickly and effectively buried.

I suspect too that it was because Manley cared so much about his international reputation, why he agreed to the opposition's demand for an election to be held in 1980, a year before it was legally required to be held.

Incidentally, John Hearne the columnist to whom I referred above had been Michael Manley's best friend for decades. However, when he saw the brutality that Manley's government was wreaking against those who did not support their party and the crawling communism they were trying to inflict on the country, he started to criticize the government in his columns. So, incensed did the PNP become by what they considered his "treachery" that when he attended their next conference, (he had been a card-carrying member of the party and had always attended their conferences) he was beaten mercilessly by activists there.

Because of the love of writing which I had developed in high school, I had added the use of the press to my cache of ammunition in opposition to the government. This I had started soon after I had become disenchanted with the PNP. Firstly, I launched a letter writing campaign, probably only surpassed by the late Alexander Bustamante himself. These letters which were regularly being published in the Gleaner caught the attention of the editor Hector Wynter, who offered me a weekly column in the newspaper, with pay and all.

At that time, it was popular to write under a nom de plume and I chose as mine deliberately, Kathrine G. Burgess, shortened KGB. This is because at that time, all who opposed the government were accused of being paid by the American CIA, so I thought it appropriate and hilarious even, to be writing anti-communist articles under KGB!

Incidentally, while I know of no one who was being paid by the American CIA, stories abounded that the JLP got assistance in terms of weapons and strategic advice, from their operatives. In light of the fact that those who tried to sell out our country to the eastern bloc were armed and financed by the Russian KGB and the Cuban DGI, I reiterate even now, that had the CIA or whichever other US agency not assisted the JLP in that undeclared civil war that raged between 1977 and 1980, the freedoms we accept as normal today would not have been preserved.

I have visited Cuba four times, including once in 2014 to get acquainted and spend a few days with some cousins that were born there. Although the natural beauty of that country cannot be totally destroyed, life there is simply intolerable for the residents. And I am not talking about only the lack of freedoms but also the system which makes it impossible for people to advance economically no matter how hard they work. Poverty is therefore pervasive while corruption and prostitution are rampant as people turn to any means necessary to survive.

But I didn't need to tell you that did I? For if life was not intolerable there, why would thousands of people be regularly risking their lives in rickety boats to escape from that island?

Yes, the US sanctions can be blamed somewhat for their lack of economic progress, but the communist system is designed to condemn everyone but the leaders, to a life of poverty and deprivation. Look at what is happening *today* in Venezuela!

And I say that without fear of contradiction for I visited East Germany twice before the Berlin Wall was torn down and it was like night and day when one passed between East and West Germany although the US had no sanctions against East Germany.

So, if it was the CIA that assisted us to win the battle that saved us from becoming a deprived, browbeaten and hopeless people like the Cubans, I feel nothing but gratitude towards them.

Anyway, back to the struggle.

Another weapon I chose to use, was participating in the nightly call-in program which was aired on JBC radio and hosted by PNP member Ronnie Thwaites (who later became minister of education in the PNP government).

Naturally, Thwaites was extremely biased towards the government, but I called that program almost every night to; attack the policies of the government, challenge his views, oppose the arbitrary detention of the opposition members without charge and call for their release, complain about food shortages etc. I even organized a team of women to operate from the JLP headquarters to saturate that program with dissenting calls.

It was only when I met deputy JLP leader Pernell Charles some years later, that he told me how much that type of activity had impacted the detainees. (Charles had been a very popular senior member of the JLP who was immediately detained under the State of Emergency. He was kept in solitary confinement for 11 months, only to be released without charge after the 1976 elections.)

When I met him, I was warmed by his profuse praise for us having used the radio waves nightly to shore up the confidence of the detainees, by calling for their freedom and condemning the government for detaining them for political reasons only.

He later wrote a book titled "Detained" which gave an overview of his experiences in solitary confinement at the hands of the totalitarian government and was also fulsome in his praises of the dedicated women who never forgot those detained and kept motivating them nightly via the electronic media.

In addition, I formed a paper organization called "Women Against Exploitation" and fired off news releases on just about every subject on a regular basis. This while working assiduously in the Naggo Head division in St. Catherine, at the grassroots level.

The ambition I had to become the local government representative in that division did not last long however, not because I had any problems with the seat or the people, but because of misplaced loyalty.

While I worked at the local government level, my then husband who was also a JLP activist, was working for quite a few years as caretaker of the St. Andrew West constituency where the then minister of security, Dudley Thompson of Moonex notoriety was the PNP's candidate.

However, as soon as Manley announced the date of the 1980 elections, he was unceremoniously ousted by Seaga who then installed a white man, Owen Stephenson in the seat, without even the delegates of the constituency being consulted.

This was the first but not the last time I realized that what I had heard about Seaga's leadership style was true.

My *misplaced* loyalty caused me to immediately resign my seat in protest and travel to the "Duhaney Park" section of the Constituency as this area gave strong support to the JLP. I then gathered a number of vocal supporters, informed them how Seaga had arbitrarily removed my husband and exhorted them to travel to the JLP headquarters to protest against the undemocratic action by the leader.

Yes, we did have a successful demonstration but *no,* it made no difference to Seaga what the delegates thought, so Stephenson was arbitrarily retained as the candidate.

However, despite the massive swing in the country against the Manley government which led to the JLP winning 51 of the 60 seats in the 1980 elections, Stephenson was beaten by Thompson.

The 1980 Elections

That October 5th 1980 election, which brought the communist threat to an end, was the *bloodiest* election in the history of Jamaica.

Starting on Nomination Day in February through to Election Day, the guns never ceased barking day or night as the street violence which had been ever-present for around three years, increased in *ferocity and intensity*. This not only led to more than 800 people being killed but also, thousands being injured. (As a matter of comparison, the death toll during the period leading up to the 1976 elections was 162). In addition, homes belonging to supporters and activists of both parties' island-wide were burnt to the ground and even police stations fired on as JLP and PNP supporters not only shot at each other but anyone who they thought stood in their way.

Among some innocents who were caught in the crossfire, were 153 old ladies who resided at a home for the indigent called Eventide Home. They were *burnt to death* when the home was mysteriously set ablaze on May 21st that year.

Another heart-wrenching murder was that of two, innocent young children in Top Hill, St. Elizabeth. This occurred on Heroes Day 1980, as Manley was touring the area with a group of his supporters.

According to the reports at the time, his devotees were heckled by supporters of Cecil July, an attorney who was representing the JLP in the constituency. The PNP group which was led by Manley himself, started to chase their detractors who sought refuge in a nearby home. The pursuing mob then charged the house and thinking their "enemies" were hiding under a bed in one of the rooms, fired shots wildly under the bed. When the smoke had cleared, it was discovered that it was the two young children who lived there who had been hiding under the bed and they had been shot and killed.

Tombs were subsequently erected prominently on the side of the main road near the spot where they were murdered, as a constant reminder of the day when violence rocked that quiet, deep rural community.

While the constant violence which was being perpetuated by the both sides continued, the shortage of basic foods fueled so much discontent that a growing number of members of the public joined the frequent demonstrations against the government which became more paranoid as the days passed.

One knee jerk reaction to the constant discontent was their arrest of H. Charles Johnson in June that year. He had been the leader of the insignificant Jamaica United Front Party, which had once tried to join up with the JLP. Also arrested with him were 27 members of the army all of whom the government claimed were involved in a coup attempt with Johnson. All were subsequently freed as this had only been part of the continued effort by the government to keep the country on edge with their constant cry of "destabilization".

They had a great deal of help pushing this line too, from the media houses that their activists controlled, the Press Association of Jamaica, the Jamaica Council of Churches which had adopted the so-called liberation theology, and the

University of the West Indies where most of the lecturers were allegedly communist activists.

On Election Day 1980, despite the constant violence; the shooting up of communities and polling stations, that did not prevent approximately 87% of the voting population from turning out, as the vast majority of Jamaicans were determined to get rid of Manley and remove forever the communist threat his regime dangled ominously over the island.

There were however reports of massive corruption and voter fraud being carried out by activists from both parties in many constituencies, in terms of ballot stuffing, ballot stealing and voter intimidation in communities and at the polling stations, but it was also clear that the results reflected the will of the majority.

The final results were: the JLP getting 58.9 per cent the popular votes and the PNP, 41.1 per cent of the 860,746 votes cast.

While there have been several excuses made by apologists over the years as to why the PNP was so badly routed, with the ever-present claim of
"destabilization" being the most used, it was clearly much deeper than that. For the departure from the hierarchy of the PNP of persons such as; David Coore, a former deputy prime minister; former finance minister Eric Bell; and one of the brilliant minds, Vivian Blake, who Manley defeated for the leadership of the PNP on February 9, 1969, caused many

former PNP supporters to realize that the direction the party was taking was indeed detrimental to Jamaica's interest.

That compounded with the threatening public utterances of the brash, arrogant and dangerous Cuban Ambassador Ulises Estrada, were more than enough warning for those who were not hardened communists, so former PNP supporters defected to the JLP in droves.

Out of Evil Cometh Good

I spoke about my *misplaced* loyalty above in reference to giving up my seat to protest the treatment of my ex-husband by the JLP leader. I only became aware of how misplaced that loyalty had been when my ex-husband, surreptitiously, moved right in shortly after, to take over that same parish council seat I had given up for him!

He won it when the local government election was held in 1981. And while I would not say his dishonest act led to the immediate breakdown of my marriage, it did sound the death knell to an association that had barely limped on for years. For to me, *loyalty is everything.*

But as they say, out of evil cometh good, for had I remained with the JLP and won the seat, I could never have survived long in that party under Seaga's leadership. For having had my initial exposure to politics in the PNP where young people were encouraged to put forward ideas and let their voices be heard, I soon found the JLP's way of doing things totally intolerable, briefly summarized by Seaga as "my way or the highway."

As much as I had come to dislike the turn Michael Manley made in the 70's and his determination to *sell out* the interest of Jamaicans to the Cubans, I say without apology that he was the best political leader and motivator of people Jamaica has ever had. Problem was, he sought to lead the country in the wrong direction!

Had Manley, with his great charm and ability to convince people to do just about anything, put the interest of Jamaica first like the late Lee Kuan Yew did in Singapore, this little country of ours would probably have become the richest, most dynamic and progressive island in the Western Hemisphere.

Instead, due to Manley's corrupt policies and his desire for supreme power, our GDP was reduced by 25% and high inflation became the order of the day. Also, under Manley, negative social practices such as praedial larceny (renamed capturing) were sanitized by powerful political activists aligned to the ruling party, thus driving thousands of productive farmers out of that business.

Such adverse practices which were celebrated during that turbulent period, have contributed greatly to Jamaica today becoming a *beggarly* nation with the third highest rate of indebtedness in the world, the largest gap between the rich and poor and to top it all, a country where rampant violence and corruption prevails so that "those who play by the rules get shafted." (A direct quote from Dr. Peter Phillips, a former deputy prime minister!)

Perception is not (always) Reality

According to the late American politician, Lee Atwater, "Perception is reality". This is often true as far as most people are concerned, but there are important exceptions to that rule.

I have had to deal with a number of perceptions over the years, about who I am, mostly because of some of my high-profile activities in the late 70's. Most of these perceptions were uncomplimentary of course, but as I was taught *Aesop's* fable about the man and the donkey from a very young age by my late, great, grandmother Mary Marshall, aka Schoolie, I have never cared too much or been otherwise affected by what people say or think about me.

There are two erroneous but really hilarious public impressions of me however which have lingered from the 70's and which, no matter how I have tried to explain that they could not be further from the truth, have remained intact in many quarters. (Mainly among the older generation now though!)

The first is that I was an outstanding road blocker and the second, to a lesser extent, is that I am a super "shotta!" (Markswoman!)

The late, extremely popular former Prime Minister Michael Manley, having introduced road blocking during the JBC strike in the 1960's which I referred to earlier, set a precedent in Jamaica which has been emulated regularly from then on, because of its effectiveness.

I had however been living/studying in Canada at the time Manley was setting the pace, so had not up to 1979, learnt or even heard much about this effective tactic designed to get the powers that be to pay attention to the issues that concern dissenters.

To date, no road block has ever been more successful in the history of Jamaica, than the famous/notorious gas strike which shut down the entire country from the 9th–11th January 1979.

This is an event for which numerous Jamaicans have blamed/praised both my ex-husband and I, for years.

Fact is though: I have never blocked a road in my life!

That incident took place when I was a young activist attached to the Jamaican Labour Party (JLP) after switching my allegiance from the left-leaning Peoples National Party (PNP) which my family had always supported.

At that time, my membership to the party had been through the youth-affiliate called the Nationalist Patriotic Movement (NPM) which had been conceptualized by JLP executive member Pernell Charles. Charles had been the most senior member of the JLP to have been detained without cause during the corrupt State of Emergency of 1976. It was after he was released after being incarcerated for almost a year that he came up with the idea of establishing an activist youth arm for the party.

Although I did not know Charles or in fact anyone from the hierarchy of the JLP personally, that State of Emergency demonstrated just how much Manley craved supreme power and that obvious signal could not be ignored.

Like much of the rest of Jamaica at the time, members of the newly formed organization had also become extremely perturbed by this development which had put supreme and arbitrary power in the hands of the politicians and their minions in the police force and army.

This was a time too when the economy had started to decline rapidly leading to frequent power cuts and chronic shortages of basic items including gasoline, thus causing people to sometimes have to literally *fight*, to get their hands-on basic necessities. (a la Venezuela today!)

In the meantime, the political rulers lived in splendor as they lauded their vulgar material wealth and status over us. For while we could hardly get the basics to send our children to school, stories about the luxuries that the children of politicians displayed at school were widespread as were the stories of the fabulous parties hosted by their parents.

In 1979, I had two young children, Thor, age 8 and Michele, 6 and was living in Spanish Town, St. Catherine, on a farm where we cultivated rice.

The straw that broke the camel's back came in January 1979 when another increase in the price of gas, which would have again led to another spate of increases in everything from public transportation to bread, was announced. (Incidentally, gas was then being sold for $3.00 per gallon; the tax included in the price at the time was $1.70. Today the average price of gas exceeds $500 per gallon of which a huge slice is tax!)

When the latest tax was announced, although we were few in numbers, we of the NPM decided that we had enough and were going to demonstrate in Half Way Tree Square the following Monday morning.

I don't remember how contact was made with a sitting Member of Parliament, Douglas Vaz, but we had a joint meeting the Saturday before, at his constituency office at Shortwood Road. That meeting was attended by about 300 people, most of whom enthusiastically encouraged us to go ahead with the plan and assured us that they would join in.

Early on the following Monday morning, I jumped on my small 50 cc Suzuki motorcycle and rode to Half Way Tree Square (now called Mandela Park in honor of the great Nelson Mandela himself). Half Way Tree is basically mid-town Kingston and an area through which most working people must pass. That is where we had agreed to gather and collect the placards which we had laboriously constructed and painted on the previous Saturday and hid in the park.

There were hundreds of placards as we expected a horde of protestors. Lo and behold however, when I arrived at the park at about 7 am, there were only ten other persons there to carry the hundreds of placards we had. We waited and waited for the masses to arrive, thinking it was only a matter of "Jamaica Time," but no one else turned up.

About half an hour later, we were encouraged by one of the other members of the small group to go out into the traffic anyway and march with the most relevant placards.

Full of trepidation, we hesitantly ventured out, everyone but me walking up and down on the sidewalk with the placards while singing and chanting. I couldn't leave my bike unprotected, so started to push it up and down between the traffic, begging motorists to help me buy some gas for my "non-guzzler," as the increased price threatened to put even me on my feet permanently!

While some people nodded their support or honked their horns approvingly, the public was just not prepared to join us in any protest. I now think we were not getting any support because it was a period when extreme political violence was being practiced against anyone who criticized the government and people were genuinely afraid of being attacked.

So, while most motorists would give us covert winks and prod us on, they were no takers when it came to joining us on the streets or even taking one of the numerous placards that we had on the sidewalk, to display in their vehicles.

As the minutes passed turning into what seemed to be many hours with very few persons joining to swell our numbers, suddenly a JOS bus (government owned bus) travelling west down Hope Road, the main corridor, drove up and stopped in the middle of the road beside where some demonstrators were gathered. The door then opened and what appeared to be about a dozen young men, poured out of the bus into the road.

153

Next, I saw a young man pull an ice pick from his pocket and drive it into all four tires of the bus, instantly demobilizing the vehicle. Naturally, with the huge bus blocking that major corridor, all traffic coming down Hope Road, immediately came to a stop.

As vehicles started to pile up in the road, passengers poured into the area on foot in droves, some cursing us for disrupting their lives, while others happily congratulated us for the initiative and joined in, knowing they would have to be paid for work that day as their inability to get to their jobs, would be argued as being no fault of theirs.

As our spirits soared with the sudden support, the driver of a blue Rover car tried to go through the blockade and an arrogant man pointed to a black robe hanging in the back of his car, shouting "Let me through, I am a judge and have to get to court in Spanish Town." All I heard after that was a hoarse laugh as the man with the ice pick stuck it into the four tires of his car too, declaring *"Judge, you not going to sentence anybody today."*

I have no recollection as to whether the judge fled or resignedly walked away when he witnessed the brazen assault on his vehicle, but that gave us one more immobilized automobile to block the thoroughfare and prevent any other vehicles from proceeding down Hope Road.

As Half Way Tree Square became tightly sealed like a sardine can, we were told that news flashes were coming over the radio reporting that persons were coming out in *every* district and town in Jamaica and blocking the roads also.

Success more than we could ever have anticipated!

Then the bad news came later that people all over the island had turned what was supposed to be a protest over rising prices, into a money-making affair by charging people to drive through the road blocks.

Even I had the experience but refused to pay, telling the road blockers who I encountered that I was one of the people who started the protest so I was not paying to ride my bike through any road block. This was around *11 am* and I had to travel back to Spanish Town to check on my young children who had been left at home with the helper.

My first experience was at the intersection of Dunrobin Avenue and Molynes Road where I found a tight road block with burning cars and logs, manned by men demanding money to let me through. They even hostilely tried to prevent me from finding a way around the blockade by riding through every possible gap on my small bike but finally relented after my bold declaration. I had another similar confrontation on Duncan's Pen Road just a few yards from my farm gate.

That road block against the increasing price of gas was so successful that it lasted for three days. Even now some thirty odd years later, people see me and sometimes remind me how terrible a time they had in Kingston, trying to find somewhere safe to park their vehicles as they were forced to continue their journey home, sometimes for miles, on foot on the first day.

By the second day, most Kingstonians solved the problem of not being able to get around by just staying home. Most did not mind however as they were in sympathy with the cause. Anyway, who did not want an unplanned holiday?

Besides, as business people and school administrators had seen the gravity of the situation on the first day and the determination on the faces of protestors, they thought it wise to air announcements on radio informing all that their establishments would be closed.

So, the roads blocks continued island-wide on day two, especially as word had spread overnight about how easy it was to make money by charging motorists to pass!

However, by then most motorists had wised up too and parked their vehicles at home.

By day three, the government had enough of us and sent in their armed goons and their gestapo (police) to beat up people, teargas groups, break heads and dismantle road blocks wherever they were or where they saw groups of people gathered who seemed to be waiting for an opportunity to reinstall blockades. Many of the goon squads were led by senior officials of the ruling party and of course the police who were not directly involved in beating up and teargassing people, looked on approvingly as the political thugs rained blows on demonstrators.

It was the reports of such brutal assaults on, and injury to demonstrators all over the island by armed gangs affiliated to the ruling party, which inspired one of Jamaica's leading journalists, the late Ken Jones, in his regular column in the "Star" under the theme "Life's Like That" to comment in part, a few days later;

"The demonstrations are over, at least for the time being and life is back to normal with its ever-rising prices, the shortages, the unemployment, the hopelessness and the frustrations; the government's glib excuses for persistent failure; the anguished cries of the poor and pleas for patience issued by the well-heeled members of the PSOJ. (Private Sector Organization of Jamaica.) The government with the support of violent goons and what appears to be the tacit approval of the police have cleared the way and we can all now proceed in peace along the broad road that leads to destruction."

"I think it is now time they explain how it is that a prominent PNP official was allowed to parade himself in a tense moment of political party rivalry, armed with a gun and in command of a mobile gang intent on beating demonstrations. ..."

Even today, every now and then I run into quite a few of the people who still have visible scars of the beatings they received on that day and coincidentally, the senior official referred to above by Ken Jones, is today often heralded as a highly respected "role model" and businessman!

The funny thing is that while the newspapers and radio reports credited the *entire* NPM for the successful protest, people started to single out myself and my ex-husband as the real instigators.

I suppose it was because we were the only married couple on the front-line from day one, besides a Gleaner reporter had interviewed us and ran a huge story with both our pictures on

157

their front page. The article, written by the late journalist/attorney at-law, Arthur Kitchin, was accurate in that it said we were part of the group of eleven that started it all, but I guess because of our picture on the front page, a lot of people did not bother to read the article in its entirety.

And that is why for years so many Jamaicans have perceived *me* as being a super-road blocker, despite my protests that I have personally never blocked a road in my life!

Of course, there were some people who were extremely upset at the inconvenience the three days of road blocks had caused them personally and many told me over the years how they were upset with me from then on, for messing up their lives.

One of those persons was my own late mother. She had driven to Kingston from St. Elizabeth (a distance of around 100 miles) to conduct business and had planned to return home the same day but because of the island- wide road blocks she couldn't.

I subsequently received a long lecture from her about the disruptive turn my life was taking and how inconsiderate I had been not to have warned her of our plans to bring the country to a halt.

Poor me, for I had no such plan and no idea that the simple demonstration we had schemed to mount by walking around with some placards, could have blossomed into such a monstrous event, but that is what happens when there is wide public discontent....the proverbial lighted match!

As to blocking a road, it's not that I did not try once during the three days to block the road on a lone motorist, but was not even successful.

It was on day two of the demonstration. I, along with a couple friends, was manning the Constant Spring corridor just above Half Way Tree to keep hostile people out of the square. But as persons did not want a repeat of the hardships and inconveniences, they had suffered the day before, we really did not have much to do.

Suddenly we saw a lone car proceeding slowly down the road towards us, and immediately jumped into action to stop it. The vehicle was being driven by a white man, which caused us to instantly become even more alert, as we figured he might have been a Cuban.

As we approached the car, the driver held up a single crutch saying he was on the way to the hospital. We were just about to let him through when I noticed that the license disc pasted on the windshield said "Embassy of the USSR" which meant he must have been a KGB agent!

Well that was like waving a red flag in front of a bull for you will recall that at that time in 1979, Russians and Cubans were the sworn enemies of freedom-loving Jamaicans as their agents were active in the island and we realized their activities were a direct threat to our liberty and freedoms. For, remember, it was accepted then by all that the Michael Manley government had been armed by and was getting open support from the Russian KGB and Cuban DGI.

Seeing a Russian agent therefore was like a gift from God for we were determined to drag him out of his car and give him a thorough whipping, although he was claiming to be in need of medical attention, showing us a crutch and indicating that he was going to the hospital.

He immediately realized that his ruse was not working, so quickly slammed his car into reverse, floored the accelerator and sped off backwards up Constant Spring Road before we could even move.

That frustrated my only attempt to actually block a road and live up to my reputation!

But as they say, perception is reality, so the facts as outlined will probably remain irrelevant as far as those who still hold me partly responsible for the 1979 road blocks are concerned!

Incidentally, it was ironic that during the successful gas strike in 1979, Manley himself delivered a national address on radio, condemning the road blocks and declaring in part;

> *"Look at the road blocks. They are all designed to try to cause economic dislocation...."*

Wow, I wonder what the road blocks Manley himself had organized in the 60's were designed to do? But then, why am I wondering when hypocrisy was Manley's most notable trait!

The other perception which has been accepted as reality by a lot of persons, especially in the Spanish Town area, was that I was a great heroine who shot and killed a man in my bed! No matter how often I have tried to correct this *perception,* it remains *reality*, even now to a number of persons.

The fact is, although I grew up seeing my father with a long double-barreled gun which he used for bird shooting; I suppose it was how my mother used that gun which led me to never want to have anything to do with those weapons. I did marry a man who was into guns however and on two occasions, at his insistence, I tried to learn to shoot.

On the first occasion, we had gone by boat over to Big Goat Island, a cay off the coast of Old Harbour Bay, in St. Catherine, as guests of a friend of ours who had been enlisted in the Jamaican Coast Guard. We had gone to spend the weekend, sleeping in a large tent that the army had erected there for their training exercises.

Naturally, the men could not pass up an opportunity at target practice on an uninhabited island far from the maddening crowd, and insisted that I join in.

At that time I had been a big fan of cowboy movies which made shooting appear so easy. So when my time came to shoot, I took one of the revolvers, got down on my stomach (as I had seen John Wayne do in the movies), aimed at a lizard and fired. Well that gun ricocheted and gave me such a wallop on my forehead that I can still feel the pain, and never touched a gun again for many, many years.

However, during the late 70's, murders started to become a major problem in Jamaica to the point where people were even migrating in droves just to try and keep their families safe. As I was a political activist at the time and on the front-line so to speak, I decided to take the repeated advice of my many concerned friends and family members, to get a gun for my protection.

I went to the proper authorities and did the necessary paperwork but was told I would have to go to the Rifle Range on Mountain View Avenue, learn to shoot and get a certificate of competence, before I could get a license to buy a gun. (To get a gun illegally, *then or now*, all you need is the cash or find a politician to give you one free!)

Anyway, off I went to the range. Problem is I did not know I was suffering from low blood pressure at the time and one of the effects of that condition is fainting for no apparent reason. Well to my embarrassment, as I went to the target room, put up my target, returned to the shooting section and prepared to shoot, I fainted!

I was the only woman there at the time and when I came to, I could hear the men laughing and commenting on how typical it was for women to react to the sound of gun shots by fainting.

Embarrassed, I could have buried myself when I heard them chatting and laughing and immediately lost all interest in getting a gun and never returned to the range or used a gun again.

So, when a man was killed in my bed and I was hailed as the heroine who did it, I was shocked, for I was totally incapable of any such feat and in fact, had slept through the entire frightening event. But few people who heard the real story

162

were prepared to believe the facts. I hope it is not because they all consider me "a pathologically mendacious" person but rather because perception is reality!

During the violent civil war period, although reports of death and injury had become commonplace, there were two murders, one extra chilling and one which struck home, which made me decide that I had to get my young children out of Spanish Town as it was too close to Kingston which had become, the prime killing field in the region.

The first was the report about the blood curdling murder of a young woman who was some eight months pregnant. Her body had been found in a gully somewhere near Spanish Town Road in Kingston and the baby had been cut from her stomach and thrown down beside her!

When I heard about it I was sick to my stomach for days, as I just could not comprehend how, despite our political differences, we had developed such hatred and coldness towards each other that such a vicious act could have been perpetuated against a woman.

That is when I also started to wonder if the politicians were giving their gunmen coke or some other mind-altering drug to numb their senses, thus causing them to carry out such atrocities without compunction.

The other incident was the murder of a couple I had just met at a party the night before. I think their surname was McIntosh or maybe it was McDonald. They lived somewhere in the Eastwood Park area of Kingston and the wife had been a long-serving PNP supporter and political activist, working with the David Coore team. Coore was a former deputy prime minister in Manley's government.

Like so many people who did not like Manley's closeness with the Cubans and the direction he was trying to take the country, she and her husband had switched allegiance and immediately started to work with the JLP, hoping to stop the government in its tracks.

I had met them at a party the Saturday night and we struck up an instant friendship as we had so many stories to share about having been an activist in one party and moving over to the other almost straight away.

I therefore could not believe my ears when I got a telephone call the next day relating how they had both been murdered early that morning. From what I heard, although their house was fully grilled, gunmen had spent quite a long time sawing off a section of the steel grill. Apparently on hearing the gunmen outside, the couple had sought refuge under the bed but that did not help as they were both found shot up with dozens of bullets as they hugged each other tightly.

That one really struck home and sent a streak of fear straight down my spine as I had only been speaking to them just a few hours before.

At that time, my mom still lived in the community where I was born, quiet, remote Malvern in the parish of St. Elizabeth, far away from Kingston.

However, Malvern was only about ten miles from Southfield where Manley and his goons had killed the two young children a few weeks before. That was considered an aberration though, as the murder was committed by gunmen from a garrison in Kingston, whom Manley had taken on his trek into the country.

Incidentally, it was not unusual for Manley to take gunmen from the garrisons on his trips, the most notorious case being when he took a vicious killer called "Feathermop" to Cuba on one of his visits there.

Feathermop was murdered shortly after returning to Jamaica as it was alleged that he had "overstepped his place" and insulted a highly placed female member of Manley's entourage, while there.

Anyway, I felt my children would be safer in Malvern and told my ex-husband that this would be the best place to send them until the war was over.

We took the 100-mile journey and explained the situation to my mom, who was only too happy to have them living with her. (There were no house telephones in Malvern at the time). We then went to the nearby Munro Prep school and had them registered there.

It literally broke my heart to have to return home without them, but what choice did I have? It was really a heart wrenching decision as they cried uncontrollably when we told them they had to stay in the country for a while.

We tried to visit often, but because of the gas shortage at the time, sometimes it was weeks before we could see them again. And every time the traumatic scenario was played out at each parting, for it was as if a cold hand grabbed my heart all over again as they wept uncontrollably and I could not even comfort them as I was crying even more than they were. But as hard as it was, we just had no choice.

And as fate would have it, that was indeed a wise choice.

I was and still am, probably the heaviest sleeper in the world and nothing, but nothing wakes me up quickly, even today.

One fateful night, I had been alone at home at the farm in Spanish Town and recall vividly; I had been listening to a radio call-in program being moderated by the late Dick Pixley. The last time-signal I heard was 10 pm. I fell asleep before my ex-husband came home so when he arrived, I was in dreamland.

When I awoke though, I thought I was having a nightmare in slow motion and real color, for there was a man in a mask on top of my ex-husband, right there beside me in *my own bed.*

I remember dazedly asking what was happening for I guess I still thought I was dreaming. It must have been the tone of my ex-husband's voice that brought me to reality for he shouted, "Don't you see a man on top of me."

Immediately I became conscious enough to realize that indeed there was a man in a mask in my bed on top of him and blood was everywhere. The entire bedroom was also in total confusion because while I slept, the two men had been wrestling for control of the gun, right there on the bed beside me and even the radio, which had been on a bedside table

166

when I was listening to it, was entangled with other stuff on the bed.

During the struggle, my ex-husband had been chopped by the machete and also shot while other bullets had found their mark in the intruder, but none of that woke me up earlier at all. When I finally became aroused, five shots had already been fired and the gun was empty.

I referred to the wise choice we had made by sending the kids to the country, for the intruder had entered through a window in *their* room and God knows what he would have done to them had they been there.

He had apparently spent some time wandering around the house too, before entering our bedroom. That is how he got the machete for he had obviously broken into the house carrying only a knife. We had bought that shiny machete in Mexico and as it came sheathed in a beautifully decorated leather case, we had mounted it as a souvenir on the wall in the sitting room.

Since he had arrived armed with only a knife as a weapon, apparently when he saw the clean, shiny machete, he had figured it would be more effective. So, he had wrapped up the knife in newspaper and pushed it into the waist of his pants, and when he entered our bedroom, he was swinging the machete.

All this we surmised after it was all over. We also subsequently learnt that the intruder had recently received bail from the Gun Court and had told quite a few people that he wanted a gun to kill the policeman who had locked him up.

It was pretty well known around Spanish Town that the owner of our farm had a gun as he did a lot of target practice on the property. So that is why he had picked our home.

Unfortunately for the intruder, his target had not yet fallen asleep so when he entered the bedroom, my ex-husband saw him, immediately grabbed his gun from under his pillow and started shooting. As he fired, the man had jumped on him on the bed and started chopping.

As they fought beside me, I slept peacefully.

By the time I got awake; my ex-husband had been shot in one hand and chopped on his foot while the man had two or three bullets in his chest. Since the gun was a five shooter, I can only surmise that the other bullets had landed elsewhere in the room or maybe even in the bed on which I slept.

When I had finally realized what was happening and grabbed the man, he barely moved as he was already half-dead, so he fell helplessly on to the bed.

There was blood everywhere, all over the bed, on the walls and even all over the radio which had fallen on the bed during the struggle.

Although dazed, I remember seeing blood all over my night clothes too but now, can't remember if I stopped to change them. I don't remember picking up the gun and the machete either, but clearly, I did as everyone told me that when I entered the emergency room at the hospital, I had the gun in one hand and the machete in the other. Don't ask me either, how I drove with a weapon in each hand, for clearly, I had operated on "automatic pilot" all the way!

What I still remember vividly was the great fear that overcame me at the thought of having to go outside in the dark, when I realized that I had to take my wounded husband to the hospital. For I had assumed the man had not come alone but had accomplices waiting for him outdoors. And it was super dark as our nearest neighbor was about a half mile away.

Only god knows how I got through that night but it certainly wasn't me who shot the man. For I am no heroine and I still had not held a gun since that embarrassing incident at the rifle range when my low blood pressure had caused me to faint.

The more I denied being a heroine to the people who came up to me in Spanish Town however, the more the rumor spread that I was a super "shotta." (I was great with a gun.) While I understand why my carrying the weapons into the hospital could create that impression, the truth is I was not totally aware of what I was doing and had operated on remote.

When we had seen that the man had gone to the trouble of putting on a mask, we had assumed he had been one of our workers. As it turned out, he wasn't, but in fact had been an attendant at the station where we purchased gas in Spanish Town. He must have expected that we would have recognized him, but we didn't. I understand his mother refused to take possession of his body and we were not even required to attend coroner's court.

As to sleeping like the dead, after that night, I just couldn't close my eyes at nights for at least a month. For each time I did, I kept seeing a man in a mask on my bed. After a few years however it was back to the dead zone, thank heavens as I really enjoy being out of it!

I never lived at that house in Spanish Town again either, although we returned there once and I tried to sleep but couldn't. That night, I decided I would never live at the farm again. Happily, though, I have resumed my habit of sleeping like the living dead and still continue to enjoy the bliss of deep, sweet sleep.

Post 1980

I don't know if I had naively expected life to be "happy ever after" when we got rid of Manley, the Cuban/Russian influence, and defeated the communists who would have totally wrecked our economy and deprived us of our freedoms.

However, that hasn't been our reality and I now often wonder if Jamaica will ever get out of the economic quagmire that we have put ourselves in, or remove the hangover in violent behavior caused by our power hungry politicians who have created/operated garrisons.

For our most powerful, power hungry politicians have now become accustomed to having garrisons which give them the

170

easy route to power. (Via violence and intimidation instead of hard work in the trenches).

As they are the only ones with the real power to change things, are there any who will work against their own interest by bringing an end to garrison politics?

I see no indication that any have the people's interest at heart to the degree that they will make this bold step.

So, with all studies indicating that the garrisons are *the* cradles in which most of the numerous psychopaths have been born and nurtured, what hope can we hold out for peace to ever prevail in our tiny country without exemplary and patriotic political leadership?

For, if one is to believe Dr. Charles' 2016 report mentioned earlier, not only did it find that the number of garrisons have been increasing but it also supported previous findings about the incubation of Jamaica's severe problem with violence, which seems positioned to get worse not decrease .

> *".... the study measured psychopathy among a cohort of shooters from two violent garrison communities in Jamaica to understand the psychological characteristics of these killers who drive the country's high homicide rate and undermine democracy."*

And concluded;

> *"....... the shooters' environmental experiences lead to the development of psychopathic personalities, resulting in their deadly actions."*

Based on the evidence in front of us, there can no longer be any doubt that the majority of Jamaican murderers are indeed vicious psychopaths, since it has almost become a practice among many, to even murder women and children when the prime targets cannot be found or evade them.

Dr. Charles is also correct in my view, when in his report, he went on to lay the blame for this terrible development that continues to bedevil our beautiful island, squarely into the laps of the politicians who represent or have created garrisons. (We have sixty-three constituencies and his conclusion that 21 politicians must bear the blame, implies that approximately a *third* of our constituencies are now either full-blown garrisons or have dangerous garrison areas within them. If he is correct, it means this murderous political tendency is increasing not diminishing, as for years the number of garrisons or near garrisons stood at 25%)!

Also, apart from us being among the top five murder capitals in the world, we are also now among the top three most indebted countries with a full 20% of our population living in poverty, some 200,000 suffering from malnutrition and the largest gap between rich and poor in the western world.

These troubling statistics have caused me at times to look back at the struggles of the 70's and wonder if it was worth the effort.

However in 2014, I returned for another visit to Cuba and on seeing how depressing it was, not only because the communists there have been so successful in achieving a total distribution of poverty, but also because people have no personal freedoms, I say with full confidence, yup, despite our present difficulties, *it was worth the effort.*

For while Jamaicans can hop on a plane to go wherever we wish whenever we want, as long as we have the money, my heart broke when an elderly cousin in Cuba told me there was nothing she wished more than to be able to visit the homeland of her parents which is only 90 miles away but she couldn't as she did not even have a passport! (Getting a passport there I hear is almost mission impossible, even if you have the money to pay the high cost.)

So, what really happened after 1980 to put us in Jamaica on the economic dung hill?

We know that the Manley era which ended in 1980, left us with a 25% slump in our GDP as the socialist government had gone through a phase of distributing the nation's wealth to their supporters without ever requiring them to produce anything. Also, the massive corruption during that era took its toll in addition to the nationalization of commercial enterprises and the fleeing of the business class, who took not only their money with them but also their entrepreneurial skills.

But this is now 2016, so why over 30 years later, we are still unable to make economic progress?

Edward Seaga who became prime minister in 1980 after the Manley disaster years was a fairly good economic manager and will probably go down in history as Jamaica's best minister of finance. For when he took over, the Jamaican economy was virtually in shambles.

Further, because of our brave anti-communist struggle and victory, Seaga had earned the respect of Ronald Reagan, the then US president, who went overboard in pouring aid into this little country. In addition, through his own initiative, Seaga had put measures into place to attract Asian investors in the garment industry, thus creating some twenty thousand jobs especially for women, in the short run.

By the mid 80's the economy had started to experience growth and the chronic shortages which had bedeviled us up to 1980, (a la Venezuela today) had long become a thing of the past. GDP declined by 4.5 per cent in 1985 but between 1986-1988, it averaged 4.8% growth.

Then came Hurricane Gilbert in 1988, the most devastating hurricane to hit the country in over 30 years.

It left damage estimated to be in excess of 4 billion US dollars. With that crushing setback, the Seaga government just could not keep the promise of economic deliverance that they had made while in opposition.

Besides, with Seaga's dour personality he just could not connect well with the Jamaican people, so dissent increased rapidly.

On the other hand, by 1989, the very charismatic Michael Manley had taken his time in opposition to remake himself into an unapologetic capitalist, even asking forgiveness from the Jamaican people for the experiment of the 70's which had caused so much chaos.

Top organizers in PNP had also gone back to square one and worked strategically into making their party an election winning machine.

In the meantime, after the 1980 elections, the JLP headquarters had been virtually closed down and most political activity ceased. What I found particularly despicable too, was that when rare meetings were called, party members had little or no voice in any of the discussions. These in fact became nothing but occasions where Seaga's dictates were passed on without any input or discussion from the floor. That caused many of the younger and independent-minded supporters to start withdrawing from party support/activity.

Further, Jamaica had always been a country with quite a subtle racial problem. So, while the vast majority of the population who were black was either very poor or terribly marginalized, the bulk of the country's wealth had always been concentrated in the hands of white or near white minority. This was because for decades, the opportunities for advancement had a built-in racial tinge, so it was always easier for lighter skinned persons to be offered opportunities, whether educational or work - related, that could propel them.

Seaga, though a white Jamaican, was extremely popular in his poor black constituency of West Kingston where he ruled with an iron hand like an overlord during colonialism. However, that leadership *style* could not wash nationally.

In fact, in retrospect, I dare say he could *never* have emerged as leader of the country had it not been for the communist threat!

For the arrogant leadership style which he displayed after he became prime minister was widely interpreted as a show of racial contempt for the broad masses of the poor black people in the country. This impression was further reinforced when many of the rich white and light skinned Jamaicans who had fled overseas during the Manley era, returned home and were appointed to positions of prominence in the government and in high- profile private sector establishments.

It is a fact that racial prejudice had been a serious problem in Jamaica before and after independence.

However, it had receded a bit during the 70's but had once again started to subtly raise its head in the 80's.

Seaga's arrogance and refusal to communicate with vast majority of the people therefore fueled that perception' and gave the PNP an easy angle to exploit as they were able to paint his refusal to be accountable and communicative as being nurtured by disrespect for black people.

Although, the economy had declined during the 70's, social legislation benefitting the masses had been enacted during Manley's tenure and that endeared the majority to him anyway.

Also, Seaga's government had set out to reform the economy using the trickle down formula, so the majority of the marginalized became extremely impatient as the economic benefits, while being very visible within most of the middle and certainly in the upper class, were not flowing down to them fast enough.

Complaints by the Manley-led opposition that the trickle-down system was not good for the majority of the people, therefore found great traction at the grassroots.

Despite all that, I remained loyal to the JLP (though not as enthusiastic as I had been during the late 70's,) until 1983, for the struggles and the dangers we had faced remained freshly etched in my consciousness.

Then I went to the JLP conference in 1983.

At the time I had a very close friend who was a JLP member of parliament. His name was Neville Lewis. He was also a minister of government but more importantly, had deep roots in my parish, St. Elizabeth and I had known his family from birth as his parents had been close to my paternal grandmother.

As a western Jamaica man, (St. Elizabeth is located in the west of Jamaica) he was very popular with delegates of the party in that region and for the upcoming conference; they encouraged him to run for the post of Deputy Leader.

When the party leader heard about it, in his true dictatorial style he mandated that there should be no challenges for the post as HE wanted the incumbent four deputy leaders to be returned *en bloc*.

By then a growing number of persons were tired of his "one don" attitude and prodded Lewis to stand up to him. The day before the election, Seaga summoned Lewis and again warned him not to run but on the day of conference, he was nominated from the floor and accepted the nomination.

I have never seen a worst example of undemocratic behavior than at that conference in 1983. This from a party which had for years, been telling the Jamaican people that they believed in democracy and totally rejected dictatorship.

At those internal elections which were held at the National Arena, I personally saw humble delegates from the peaceful Jamaican countryside being terrorized by Seaga's supporters from his garrison in Tivoli Gardens.

They threateningly demanded that the delegates not vote for Lewis. Where delegates stood their ground, the garrison activists even seized the ballots and tore them up right in front of them. It was a most shocking display.

When I challenged an influential lady from Tivoli Gardens whom I knew, I was taken aback when she claimed that *they* really wanted Lewis to win but the leader had said he did not want him!

This happened on a Sunday and at the end of it all, despite voter intimidation and malpractices, when the ballots were counted, Lewis was ahead by 14 votes. As the count was so close, Seaga said he would not accept the results and soon it was announced from the platform that because the outcome was so tight, there had to be a recount. Then came the announcement over the microphone which was a real shocker;

> *"As it is late, the ballots will be stored at the JLP headquarters for recounting on Monday morning".*

I immediately realized that based on what we had seen, that was most likely a ploy to swop or destroy some ballots over the weekend so Lewis would be declared the loser. Therefore that night on returning home, I immediately took matters into my own hands by calling the Radio Jamaica (RJR) newsroom *anonymously* and told them:

> *"Despite extensive bogus voting at the JLP conference today, Neville Lewis won the race for deputy leader by a small margin of 14 votes."*

This was carried verbatim in their 7 am newscast the following Monday morning and we heard nothing further about any recount after that.

For months however there were questions and speculation in the party as to who had leaked the information to the station and of course I remained silent until now, apart from confiding to Neville that it had been me!

While the mission to prevent Seaga from foisting a deputy leader on the party delegates who they did not want was successful, it never stemmed his anger or vindictiveness. Lewis was therefore sidelined as deputy leader and for as long as I can recall, I never saw his name mentioned on any of the party's advertisement where the deputy leaders were down to speak. Nor was he assigned any responsibilities as other deputy leaders were.

Seaga's leadership style and the closing down of the party's machinery could easily have caused him to become a one term prime minister, but fortunately for him, ultra-leftists in neighboring Grenada, led by the deputy prime minister Bernard Coard and supported by the Cubans and some cohorts in Jamaica, murdered Maurice Bishop, the sitting prime minister there, and seized power in 1983.

This was an immediate and vivid *reminder* to us in the entire Caribbean of the serious threat that Cuba still posed to all our freedoms. The islands therefore happily welcomed the decision by the US government under President Reagan, to invade Grenada and re-establish democracy there.

Seaga quickly took advantage of that emotional event to call snap elections in Jamaica two years before they were due. Interestingly, although the PNP general secretary Paul Robertson had for some time been challenging the prime minister to go to the polls as the people were becoming disenchanted with his leadership style, when he grabbed the opportunity the turmoil in Grenada had given him and called early elections, the PNP boycotted the polls claiming the voters list was outdated!

The JLP therefore received a temporary respite.

In 1986 when the local government elections were called, he should have gotten a good idea of what people really thought of his leadership style for in that election at the local level, the JLP was virtually wiped out. But not even then would he accept that he was passé.

His lack of respect for people in general; his intolerance of bright people who I assume he feared would show up his deficiencies; his inability to motivate even those around him to show initiative and not just take orders; led to the slow but sure disintegration of the JLP. In fact, it would not be incorrect to say that the party soon descended into a perpetual state of turmoil, with senior people leaving in droves. As members and activists departed, Seaga's paranoia increased with him constantly looking under the proverbial bed and declaring that there were schemes and "gangs" of senior persons in the party plotting his overthrow.

Of course, these constant inter-party disagreements made excellent news in the press thus as long as he remained leader of the fragmented and divided party, voters and financiers started to withdraw their support.

By 1989, when the general elections were due and called, the opposition PNP had been reinvigorated under the leadership of a supposedly-reformed Manley while the JLP had been floundering. The PNP therefore easily won 45 of the 60 seats to the JLP's 15. However, by then many people had become so disenchanted with the two leaders that voter turnout had fallen from the 87% it had been in 1980 to just over 78%. I assume it could be that despite Seaga, many "thinking" people still could not warm to Manley, regardless of his claim of having changed philosophically, so they stayed away from the polls.

Despite losing that election, the previous terrible wipeout at the local level in 1986, and the constant disintegration of the party machinery island wide, Seaga would not resign from the leadership of the party, nor could he be removed because of the fear delegates had of the dangerous activists in Tivoli Gardens.

We will never know what type of leader Manley would have become after he won in 1989 however, for after a year he resigned because of health problems.

He was succeeded by his deputy prime minister, P.J. Patterson who was always reputed to be an organizational genius. Patterson ended up becoming Jamaica's longest serving prime minister, fourteen years, but his government will be best remembered for its extreme economic incompetence under the leadership of the finance minister Omar Davies, not to mention the entrenched corruption and widespread patronage.

For during the Patterson reign, not only were the elite of the party highly rewarded from the treasury with contracts and other perks but also a small tight cadre became the extremely rich, new black ruling class, comparable only to the situation in Zimbabwe.

By keeping the dwindling resources of the country mainly distributed among the party faithful, that new PNP became even more formidable despite the economy bouncing between recession and depression. However, with the ever unpopular and paranoid Seaga leading the only viable alternative party, the Patterson regime had nothing to fear, despite very vocal criticism by the "articulate minority," concerning the failed economic policies, gross injustice in the society, rampant cronyism and corruption.

While from the mid 80's I had become totally disgusted with politics and had decided to opt out of any form of political or social activism, in 1999 when I could no longer stand quietly and watch the direction in which the country was going, I joined up with a non-political organization conceptualized by Gleaner columnist Dawn Rich, called Citizens for Civil Society. They planned a series of public demonstrations around various issues, even attacking the political leadership of both Patterson and Seaga.

Unfortunately, the well-publicized demonstrations attracted more police keen on taking our photographs to try and intimidate us I suspect, than members of the public willing to stand up for anything.

Admirably though, at the last demonstration I participated in, the late, outstanding Gleaner columnist Morris Cargill, though almost 90 years old and ailing, turned up in his wheelchair to show his solidarity.

Unfortunately, or maybe fortunately, I missed the last of the three planned demonstrations as I was not in the country. That last one was held in Half Way Tree Square but I understand it was quickly and violently broken up by JLP thugs who invaded the crowd and attacked demonstrators for calling for Seaga's resignation.

After that, I withdrew from all political and civil activity and concentrated on trying to make a living while still expressing my views through the media, as an ineffective member of the *articulate minority*.

As far as I was concerned, the fight against corruption; to improve the economy; the struggle for justice and to preserve and maintain our freedoms; should now rightfully be taken up by the younger generation as we had done against communism in our youth.

For they ought to be concerned about the future of their country as it was patently clear by then that Patterson was totally incompetent, as according to the World Bank statistics, GDP growth in most other countries worldwide was increasing steadily from 1995, while our economy was floundering.

In fact, in Jamaica, during that period, we even had a devastating collapse of the entire financial sector which naturally exacerbated the pervasive poverty already ravishing the land.

This was mainly due to the extreme corruption coupled with an ill-conceived high interest rate policy that brought down almost every bank while wiping out some 40,000 businesses in its wake.

This economic disaster was being compounded by a frightening murder rate which took us into the realms of the top five murder capitals of the world by the mid 90's, so it was totally amazing to me that Patterson was able to keep his party in power for such a long period without any serious unrest.

But I guess the alternative party under the current leader was just too unpalatable for the Jamaican people.

For despite losing four general elections, Seaga would not and could not be removed as leader of the JLP as he was propped up by unthinking loyalists supported by the *dons* who controlled his constituency in Western Kingston, whose penchant for intimidating delegates at the annual conference was very well known. Also, as any criticism of his leadership or suggestions for improving anything at all, were seen as disloyalty almost punishable by death, concerned people were just not speaking out as they should.

His political leadership of the JLP therefore was not only a blessing in disguise for the incompetent Patterson-led PNP but it also left the alternative party with mostly persons who were prepared to remain in politics simply to take orders, thus depriving the country of credible leaders who could mobilize dissenters.

As the more progressive persons continued to defect and few new young people were joining to invigorate the party, desperation and paranoia increased among the depleting top echelon and the few who propped up the leader. This led to even louder and more public contention, greater implosion and ever more massive departure of even his once most loyal supporters, each time followed by shriller claims from the leader and his sycophants, that the most recently departed had joined gangs, like the extensively reported "gang of 5" and "gang of 11," to depose him.

It is evidence of how much Seaga had turned off the Jamaican electorate that in the midst of the most massive economic collapse in the country and Jamaica gaining the unenviable distinction of becoming one of the five murder capitals in the world, Patterson, one of Jamaica's most incompetent and uncaring prime ministers, kept leading the PNP to electoral victory after electoral victory. Yes, while it is true that with each election, voter turnout diminished, the truth is that since we operate the "first past the post system", if even one person per constituency votes while the rest abstain, the party with the most seats becomes our government by default.

Jamaicans have for years been yearning for a third choice to free us from the stranglehold of the JLP and PNP; however, because of how the political system was structured and has been corrupted, it impossible for a third party to become a serious force without addressing the "elephant in the room" called Local Government.

As it stands, although this country has a very small population of only 2.8 million people, a very large percentage of our resources is being spent paying for unnecessary politicians and bureaucrats, most of whom are simply party activists dedicated to getting/keeping their party in power to control of the diminishing wealth of the nation.

So totally over governed are we that we currently operate *fifteen* governments. These are; central government plus thirteen parish councils and one municipal council, all propped up by overstaffed bureaucracies.

This over-government which the politicians have imposed on us to provide work for partisans to the detriment of the country, has caused us to rack up a public wage bill which devours 43% of government revenue. This is extremely excessive according to an IMF survey which shows that internationally, in Low Income Countries, the ratio is 26.8%, Middle Income countries 28.2% and high income countries: 25.9%.

(Source; Evaluating Government Employment and

Compensation Benedict Clements, Sanjeev Gupta, Izabela Karpowicz, and Shamsuddin Tareq. Fiscal Affairs Department, IMF)

Our local government system remains among the most corrupt institutions in the island, with councilors awarding most contracts to family, political activists (including gunmen) and friends without any accountability, so naturally taxpayers get little or no benefit from the billions of dollars spent at that level.

Also, because, like at central government, bribery and corruption have become the norms, there is no efficient governance at that level either. So for example, while the major function of local government has been set out as being "Town Planning," there is not one town that I can identify in Jamaica that is properly/attractively laid out or expanded, for all it takes is a bribe to councilors and bureaucrats at the local government level to have them overlook/approve each and every infraction.

As the local councilors who are drawn from the two dominant parties do very little work, they can spend most of their time out in the field organizing and campaigning for their respective parties at the ground level. In other words, taxpayers inadvertently pick up the tab for some 286 local representatives of the JLP and PNP island-wide, plus the bureaucrats who are usually employed on a political basis to the local councils, to conduct party activities almost 24/7.

With the two dominant parties enjoying such an advantage at the grassroots level, which third party can ever garner the resources or manpower to compete successfully against them?

Over the years therefore, while a slew of third parties have emerged, they have quickly died.

While as the JLP remained a poor alternative government, the country continued to flounder into the 21st century under Patterson's corrupt and incompetent leadership and it was not until January 2005, that Seaga who was by then almost eighty years old, was finally forced to go.

This was due to almost all once-loyal contributors and fund raisers finally refusing to finance the party any longer under his leadership. Without money to organize and few *young* energetic activists being attracted to the party, the organization was almost ready for the morgue by then.

He was quickly replaced by his former protégé, Bruce Golding who had left the party some time before as one of the "gang of 11. " On leaving, Golding had joined one of the floundering ineffective third parties, the National Democratic Movement (NDM) but was easily and quickly convinced to return to the JLP by its loyal, rich financiers and powerful fund raisers. Besides he knew from experience that third parties had no future in Jamaica and had only been marking time with the NDM.

When the next general election was held in September 2007, the JLP still had not reorganized itself properly nor managed to attract back enough credible, dynamic persons into its ranks, so despite years of devastating economic performance by the incumbent PNP, they barely won that general election by a mere four seats.

However, the new leader, Bruce Golding did not last very long as within four years he was forced to resign for putting the interest of the *super-don* Christopher Coke aka Dudus from the West Kingston garrison constituency which he had also inherited from Seaga, ahead of the country's interest. (The West Kingston constituency includes the Tivoli Gardens, described by the security forces as the mother of all garrisons.)

For those unfamiliar with these events which will most likely be soon the topic of many books as a lengthy and fulsome commission of enquiry was held into some aspects of events there, I will give a brief recap.

Although Dudus had a been a notorious law-breaker in Jamaica for decades, he was never brought to justice or even wanted by our police as the powerful political Tivioli-connection and the high level of corruption in the police force, made him *untouchable,* locally.

However, he had committed many crimes including murder, gun running and drug trafficking in the USA during a short stint there and they applied for his extradition.

He was however considered too valuable to the JLP, so the prime minister (Golding) used every means at hand to try and prevent him from being extradited. That caused a major rift with the USA government resulting in a serious local backlash among the vocal middle and business class as well as the powerful media, so Golding was forced to resign.

Meanwhile in the PNP, Patterson had resigned in 2006 when he saw that the country was totally fed up with his type of leadership and the corruption and economic devastation it engendered, so he, fearing that his beloved party would lose the next election under his leadership, stepped down.

He was succeeded by the very popular Portia Simpson Miller, Jamaica's first female party leader and first female prime minister. However even she could not save the badly discredited PNP which had been in power for 18 years but had failed to improve the lot of the people, although the rest of the world had been enjoying a long run of economic stability and growth during those years.

So, despite her great charm and popularity among the masses, the PNP still lost the 2007 election.

When Golding was forced out of office in 2011, in a most undemocratic thrust, he virtually named his young minister of education Andrew Holness as his heir, claiming the country needed new, young blood.

Holness who was 40 years old, lasted less than six weeks in office as prime minister for the backlash over the Dudus affair had injured the JLP severely. He was therefore easily defeated by the rejuvenated PNP under the leadership of Portia Simpson Miller, for despite the poor job the PNP had done in government, it had never injured Jamaica's reputation internationally as Golding had done.

As leader of the opposition, Holness quickly caused eyebrows to be raised when, despite his few years in the *working* world, he set out to build one of the largest, most imposing and ostentatious mansions in Jamaica, on top of the prestigious Beverly Hills, overlooking Kingston.

He also displayed troubling dictatorial tendencies (a la Seaga, who had been his political mentor) as it was revealed that before he had appointed the opposition senators to the upper house of parliament, he had demanded that they give him *signed, undated letters of resignation.*

The shocking revelation of that most dangerous and destabilizing act was made by a former senator Arthur Williams, an attorney at law whom he had instructed to draft the letters. Williams and another former senator Christopher Tufton, took the matter to court when they were not reappointed to the new opposition senate, charging that Holness had unconstitutionally completed the signed and undated letters and submitted them to the governor general, to deprive them of their seats in the Upper House.

To this undemocratic act, the Constitutional Court said in part about Holness" action:

> *"It is inconsistent with the Constitution, contrary to public policy and, accordingly, null and void."*

Portia Simpson Miller continued as prime minister but will probably go down in history as the worst female leader in the free world. For her regime in the main, was just a continuation of Patterson's, so mismanagement and dishonesty in public affairs, continued to strangle the struggling economy to the point where the gap between the rich and the poor in Jamaica was recorded as the widest in the western world.

Worse too, Simpson-Miller displayed such a level of arrogance that during her tenure, she seemed to have deemed it infra dig for her to account for her performance or the actions of her government, so refused to hold press conferences or answer questions any about anything including, the lack of economic progress or the troubling corruption that plagued her administration.

Instead her administration opted to feed the hunger for answers with canned information from the government's information arm, the Jamaica Information Service.

Haughtily thinking that her leadership style was only being criticized by an unimportant "articulate minority," Simpson Miller called the general election in February 2016, one year earlier than due and was shocked when her party lost by one seat. (32 JLP, 31 PNP)

However, as most Jamaicans had become disgusted with the both major parties, only 47.72 % of registered electors turned out to vote, most no doubt being the hard core, who are often dismissed locally as unthinking "diehearted" supporters.

So as the see-saw continues, the JLP's Holness is once again the prime minister of Jamaica, a poor country where today close to a million miserable souls live below the poverty line, with many of them existing in gross uncertainty in hovels built on lands to which they have no legal right. In addition, injustice is rampant as the "law is not a shackle" to anyone willing to pay off the relevant authorities to do as they please so those who play by the rules often get shafted.

Further, social services are terribly inadequate and for the very poor who have no choice but to use the deplorable public health services, it is said that for them life is like having died and gone to hell.

In fact, it was these terrible conditions in the public health sector which drove the president of The Jamaica Medical Doctors Association (JMDA) to expose some of the unbearable conditions in April 2015.

These included:

> *doctors not having proper surgical aprons and having to use plastic bags in surgery; shortage of surgical masks; doors being unable to close so flies invade operating theatres as does bacteria; leftovers from an individual's surgery are used on someone else; anesthetic machines not being properly serviced so they give inaccurate readings; no sutures; malfunctioning air-condition machines break down often so they have to end up using fans which results in sweat dripping into wounds. Then there is the perennial shortage of antibiotics and even antibacterial soap for doctors to scrub with. In addition the hospital plants are poorly maintained with termite dust on the ceilings and even falling into the wound of a patient, in one instance.*

Of course, as our politicians very rarely use our public health services, it would be a miracle in my book if there is any great improvement in the health services under the new administration anyway. For the normal ritual is that taxpayers hear by the way that a leading politician has had to go to hospital and has been taken away by air ambulance to a facility in the nearby USA. And who pays for their special treatment?

The long suffering taxpayer of course!

In general, over the past decade, there has been a steady breakdown in most services for members of the public and where laws exist for the good order of the society, they are rarely enforced against the politically privileged or well-heeled.

I therefore often wonder if things will ever really improve much for the masses in the near future, even if this new set of politicians really have the people's interest at heart. For Jamaica's real economic problems have stemmed from our politics being hijacked by greedy activists whose only mission was/is, to enrich themselves while reveling in the pomp and ceremony which are some of the perks of power in the economically deprived country.

Unfortunately, while politicians raid the treasury by giving multi-million dollar contracts to their bag men, family, friends, party activists and even their dons (some of whom have been smart enough to form private companies with innocuous names to hide their true identities), somehow they seem to have little difficulty convincing their gullible, die-hard supporters that social conditions are deteriorating because of the tight debt problem the country faces, despite the stark evidence pointing to fraud and malfeasance being the main causes.

And because political corruption has been so rife, there is very little to show for the immense debt racked up over the years, which has catapulted us into being the third most indebted country in the world. This should surprise no one as one World Bank study done a few years ago, found that the country gets only approximately 45% value from construction contracts awarded by the government. So how could we possibly progress when we receive nothing for a whopping 55% of the money spent in one identified area alone?

Naturally therefore, the country gets poorer each year despite the existence of a Contactor General department which investigates government contracts. But that organization is toothless so their findings and publication of massive corruption in central government, local government and agencies such as the National Housing Trust which is awash with funds paid in by poor contributors who get little or no benefits in terms of affordable housing, have never reached the point of bringing well connected political criminals to justice.

In the meantime, unemployment stands close to 15% while youth unemployment hovers at over 34%, almost one fifth of the population lives in poverty and according to a recent World Health report, some 200,000 suffer from chronic malnutrition.

The number living below the poverty level and those suffering from chronic malnutrition would however probably have been twice as much had it not been for remittances from friends and family abroad, whose gifts usually provide a significant bulk of the foreign exchange the country obtains each year. (Remittances to Jamaica in 2013 topped the US$ 2 Billion mark according to the Multilateral Investment Fund, member of IDB Group. This is almost 20% of our GDP)

I have never seen modern Jamaica in a worse economic state than it is has been for the past ten to twelve years.

No, there are no shortages like those which plagued us during the terrible 70"s, but only the rich can now afford much else besides the basics these days.

Anyway, in the 70's the country had hope because unlike today, there was a viable government in waiting, the JLP.

Today, no party offers a significant difference in leadership and viable third parties cannot emerge in the short run because of the built-in systems which favor the dominance of the two parties created by the *cousins*! So the sameness remains, regardless of which party forms the government.

Maybe if I saw an improvement in law enforcement, I would not feel so pessimistic about my country and the picture I paint would not be so dismal. However, with murders soaring, robberies constantly increasing, child abuse and rape pervasive and getting justice through the creaking court system seeming *almost impossible*, how can I be optimistic?

In fact, so rapidly have things been deteriorating over the past few years, that even a privileged President of the PNP Senate, Stanley Redwood migrated to Canada in the midst of Portia

Simpson's term in office, declaring that it was *the best hope for his family!*

In all the days of observing politics, I have never before seen such a highly *connected* member of a government abandoning his country for those reasons!

But I guess we must never fail to thank God for small mercies, for we can still import necessary protein from rich countries where people normally throw away such products. These are: chicken neck, fish back, turkey neck, chicken foot etc. which are now the protein staples for poor Jamaicans, so we have been saved somewhat from mass malnutrition!

You would never know how poor this country really is though, by looking at the lifestyle of the politicians who would never subscribe to a policy of "leading by example." So they, without any compunction at all, run up millions of dollars in first class overseas travel, enormous phone bills, traveling around in large convoys in expensive high level vehicles driven by the police, host super parties and in general flaunt an extremely ostentatious lifestyle while showering themselves and their party cohorts with honors galore.

In the meantime, essential professionals like teachers, nurses and doctors who can barely survive on the comparatively poor salaries they receive in the public service, are migrating in droves.

This has led to the virtual wiping out of the middle class, leaving us with basically just rich and poor and the widest gap between these two categories in the western world. And who falls into the category of the rich? Generally, politicians, their bagmen, relatives and cohorts, some police, gangsters and some businesspeople.

For the businesspeople who do indeed have the power because of their economic influence, to *force* change, seem to have now come to accept that corruption is a normal business expense and are unconcerned about the negative effect it has on the society. This is so why few eyebrows were raised in that sector when a former president of the Jamaica Chamber of Commerce declared on public radio in an interview with the late journalist Wilmot Perkins that;

> *"To succeed in business in Jamaica you have to be corrupt."*

Businesspersons, who cannot accept this new "norm" or the fact that they could never work hard and become rich or even comfortable in Jamaica *without selling their souls*, are left little choice but to seek their fortunes elsewhere.

Interestingly while political corruption has continued to flourish regardless of which party is in power, no politicians or their cronies have recently been jailed for the grand theft that often passes for *governance,* no matter how strong the evidence is. And I say "recently jailed" without fear of contradiction, as many apologists for the broken system like to point to the case of J.A.G. Smith (JAGS) a former JLP minister of Labor who was jailed *way back* in the 90's after it was exposed that he had stolen funds from farmworkers" compulsory savings.

However, JAGS did not end up in jail because of his corruption but because of his *arrogance!* For had he humbly accepted the "slap on the wrist" that former prime ministers, PNP Michael Manley and JLP Hugh Shearer had quietly agreed to, all would have been well.

Instead, inspired by hubris, he had verbally abused the most influential member of the then ruling PNP government who could have guaranteed his freedom. She decided to teach him a lesson thus breaking the unwritten "honor among thieves" pact between JLP and PNP politicians and off he went to jail.

Yes, while in opposition, politicians continue to use various platforms to outline the extremely unscrupulous practices being carried out by their opponents in government, but immediately as the roles are reversed and opposition becomes government, the unwritten pact between them seems to automatically trip in, shielding well known and previously named miscreants from paying the ultimate penalty through the prison system or even the slightest sanction.

Naturally, with no penalties being imposed, outright dishonesty is now at crisis levels. For can you believe that after the 2016 elections, the PNP general secretary tried to excuse his party's loss by citing shortage of funds to campaign with, as he said a large proportion of the *kickbacks* normally given to the party by Chinese investors had not been turned over to the party but had been hijacked by their own high level ministers!

With such open and blatant dishonesty being accepted as the norm, is it any wonder that we can barely find funds to finance critical areas such as the social, educational and health services?

So badly have things deteriorated in those areas causing severe frustration and loss of hope among ambitious Jamaicans that a National Youth Values and Attitudes survey in April, 2014 revealed that 43 per cent of youngsters under 18, and 49 per cent of young adults over 18, said they would willingly give up their (Jamaican) citizenship. Further, another survey conducted by the Network, a global group of online job boards in collaboration with the Boston Consulting Group, found that *96%* of Jamaicans are willing to move abroad for work.

Alarmingly too, the most recent statistics indicate that suicides are also on the increase (although the incidence of suicides in Jamaica has traditionally been exceedingly low), while domestic violence which some psychologists argue is often nourished by hopelessness and frustration, has reached alarming proportions.

Excuse me therefore if I sound cynical and negative as I take a hard look at my country, for my despair stems from the fact that I see no indication from either party which has a stranglehold on the country, that there will be any real concerted effort to rid the country of the corruption which is stifling our progress.

Despite all I have said though, I really believe there can be a great turn-around if Jamaica can only find *good leadership.*

Our country is an extraordinarily beautiful destination with unique natural attractions, world renowned athletes and musicians etc. So, as it is already a haven for tourists, we can have an even more booming industry if only we seriously dealt with our challenges, especially crime.

For if one is rich or has money to spend on a vacation, there is hardly a better place in the world to be than in Jamaica, where money buys all including security and justice. So, with our attractions, wonderful climate, beautiful rivers, waterfalls and beaches, top of the line hotels, proximity to the USA etc. where better to enjoy life?

The most debilitating aspect of life here is how it penalizes the *majority* of Jamaicans, who, because they are poor, they are powerless. For the fact is that if one obeys regulations/laws/rules, one is likely to be forever frustrated, persecuted, left behind and victimized. Or to put it another way as did a former deputy Prime Minister (and soon to be prime minster?) Peter Philips "Those who play by the rules get shafted."

This dire predicament that we find ourselves in is a direct result of the corruption which takes front and center stage of life in Jamaica as almost every policeman, bureaucrat and politician (at central and local government level) is for sale.

Oh yes, laws exist to address almost every possible ill in the society, but law enforcers more often than not, simply turn a blind eye when infractions are committed by those who will pay them, thus making life near impossible for those who would like to live in a country where law and order prevails or have no money to pay the corrupt.

In fact, Jamaica today reminds me of that place in the famous story which is popular in tourism circles. It goes;

A scientist who was dying was visited by St. Peter to find out where he wanted to go after the breath had gone. Being a scientist, he was not about to make a decision without doing the necessary research so he insisted on a visit to the both places before making a decision.

He found the first place extremely boring as people all dressed in white were just flying around or lolling on their wings while sipping milk and honey. So he asked to see the other.

By contrast, in the other place, all was swinging and he saw most of his friends having the time of their lives. So naturally, he chose the second.

*When the last breath left and he descended, he was met with nothing but abject misery in a terrible, hot place. There were vicious flames lapping at every corner and consuming screaming beings in its wake. Thinking there was an error, he asked to see the supervisor which turned out to be a horrible creature with a gruesome snarl for a smile. When he pointed out that this was not where he had chosen, the creature laughed loudly saying, "Don"t you know that when you **first** visited you were a tourist and now you are a resident?"*

Yes, Jamaica is absolutely wonderful for visitors and the rich who can enjoy the bounty of the land, but for the ever-dwindling middle class and the poor, it can be a virtual hell.

And I see no indication from the dominant parties which have a stranglehold on the country, that there will be any concerted effort in the *near* future, to rid the country of the corruption which is stifling our progress. For in excess of 80% of our young educated professionals, who could help Jamaica to really progress and bring new and better values to governance, refuse to remain in the country.

It is unfair to blame them however, for as I have been pointing out, Jamaica is an extremely difficult country in which to live and progress economically and one has to look about the welfare of one's family first. Besides, if a privileged "insider" like Stanley Redwood, former President of the Senate, sent such a disturbing signal about the dismal future his family would face if they did not migrate to Canada, what should "outsiders" think?

Unfortunately, too, many of the young people who remain, seem to know very little about our recent history, our struggles and where we are coming from politically so as our own great home grown philosopher Marcus Garvey warned us;

> *A people without the knowledge of their past history, origin and culture is like a tree without roots.*

They probably do not really understand therefore that if they want meaningful change, they have to agitate for it, as politicians are inclined to do nothing, unless it is in their own interest.

Concerned, patriotic Jamaicans really need to sit up and take note how much corruption is affecting our lives, for according to a recent report in the Jamaica Observer, the situation is rapidly deteriorating. They reported in part;

> *"JAMAICA has seemingly taken a step backwards in combating corruption and building integrity, having declined in the latest Corruption Perception Index (CPI), which ranks the country 83rd among the 176 countries and territories assessed in 2016. After amassing 41 points last year and being ranked 69th of 168 countries, Jamaica fell several positions to 83rd with a score of 39.*
>
> *In the assessments for 2014, 2013 and 2012, Jamaica consistently scored 38 points each year.*
>
> *On the other hand, Bahamas is the top ranked Caribbean Community (Caricom) country, rated as being the **least corrupt**, (my emphasis) according to the latest figures released by Transparency International."*

(In actual terms Jamaica dropped from 41 to 31 points. Transparency International has warned that a CPI score of less than 50 means "corruption is a serious problem in the country. It has also said that a poor CPI "signals prevalent bribery, lack of punishment for corruption, and public institutions that do not respond to citizen's needs.)

Does this finding assist us in understanding why the Bahamas which shares a similar history as we do and which has far less resources, is so far ahead of us economically causing Jamaicans to be constantly seeking a means to go there to gain employment? Simple! They have a much better handle on corruption than we do!

So, who is going to change things in our poor declining country?

The youth who were born into this deeply corrupt society and accept it is a norm? The politicians who gain wealth and power by making their beds with gunmen, lottery scammers and all who benefit the most from a deeply criminalized Jamaica? The business community, many of whom made their fortunes corruptly so have no interest in changing anything? The very poor majority who I think politicians deliberately keep undereducated so they can be easily bought or manipulated to the point that many cannot even recognize that living under the thumb of a don is only slightly better than our ancestors" plight under slavery?

Yes, unfortunately most of the very poor still see no chance of improving their lot without bowing to the wishes of the politicians, so they still go out to vote in droves as their dons dictate, while the vast majority of thinking people are boycotting the polls. No wonder the Chairman of the PNP Bobby Pickersgill felt so comfortable that he was able to refer disparagingly to those of us who criticize the corrupt as the "articulate minority."

He is correct however as this small minority has no real impact at election time so no ability to influence or change anything.

Yes, the undeclared civil war is behind us and under Seaga's leadership in the 80's, short-lived economic stability was beginning to be realized, even if it was only with slow GDP growth.

However, we have never reversed the negative labor productivity which had set in from 1973 when Manley convinced Jamaicans that the rich owed them a living so they did not have to produce. So, while other Caribbean countries steadily increased productivity, we have remained almost at the bottom in terms of per capita GDP in the English-speaking Caribbean.

When you compound this with the unacceptably destabilizing crime rate and the perpetual injustice that prevails in the society, is there any wonder there is such great frustration and loss of hope?

You know, looking back, I am now positive that had the civil war of the 70's about ideology not been so surreptitious, Jamaica would *never* have become the murder mecca that it is today. For, had it been declared, when the war was over there would have been *an open peace treaty* and the disarming of the combatants.

Look at how Rwanda has healed and moved ahead in a civilized manner!

In our case, because it was never accepted in Jamaica that we fought a civil war with both sides being armed by the overseas cold-war sponsors, politicians have continued to pretend they were not behind the mayhem of the period and insist that they do not support criminality and gunmen while their actions tell a totally different story. (Clear evidence of their continued support has been provided by the aforementioned incidents involving a few of their *super* dons such as Bulbie, Bebe, Dudus and Willie Haggart.)

It is my opinion that as long as our politicians continue to give succor and clandestine support to gunmen, lottery scammers, extortionists and other gangsters, our murder rate will never go down and our economy will never be able to grow to its full potential.

Despite the present picture however, I have to try to remain an optimist because from I first heard the phrase "*Dum spiro, spero*" as a teenager, I adopted it as a personal motto. This in English means "*while I breathe, I hope*" and although sometimes, it is hard to hope, when I see the type of progress that Rwanda has been able to achieve with good leadership after hitting rock bottom, I must insist that there is hope for Jamaica.

With our talents and wonderful resources whenever we get patriotic and ethical leadership, we can excel at everything. I know this leadership is out there somewhere among the youth.

I will probably not be around to see the turn-around but as Mahatma Gandhi said;

> "*You must not lose faith in humanity. Humanity is an ocean; if a few drops of the ocean are dirty, the ocean does not become dirty.*"

PART 2

WARMING TO JOURNALISM

Although I consider my greatest contribution to the journalism profession being that of helping my late friend Tony Abrahams develop and launch the "Breakfast Club" which *revolutionized* morning radio in Jamaica, I am and will always be a writer. For therein lies my passion. In fact, my ultimate goal is to retire from Jamaican life one day, travel the world on a consistent basis and become an international travel writer.

My only professional training in writing however was writing computer programs, a profession I embraced while living in Canada in the *olden* days, when computers were just entering the commercial world. I chose that profession because of the great salaries it was attracting due to a shortage of programmers. While it was an interesting challenge at first, as soon as I became really good at debugging programs, I got very bored with communicating with computers, as quite frankly I am really a people person.

On the other hand, writing just to express my thoughts, even if no one else reads it, has always come very naturally to me. My early exploits as a writer began while I was a junior at Hampton Girl's School where my friends used to turn to me to write their love letters to the boys they secretly admired at our brother school, Munro College!

While I have always loved to write, I never really developed depth until Jamaica's first poet laureate (since Jamaica gained independence in 1962), Mervyn Morris, introduced me to classical Literature at Munro College.

He had been a teacher there and from we entered sixth form at Hampton, we had the great pleasure of going over to Munro and doing the classes with the boys there. I sometimes swear that Mr. Morris must cringe every time he sees me approaching as I keep repeating to him how much he influenced me in that area.

My writing took off in the early 70's when I operated a children's nursery in Jamaica and because the major part of that business involved the practical nurses doing everything, I found I had a lot of time on my hands. My idle time probably became the bane of every news editor in Jamaica as I started spewing out letters on numerous topics every day.

I was however quite pleasantly surprised and excited when the then editor of the Gleaner newspaper, Hector Wynter called me one day to enquire if I did not want to get paid for my views? Wow. Boy was I ever ready, and there was no turning back from that day.

Although I was never on staff of the Gleaner, I did have the honor also of being recruited over the years to cover elections in Haiti, Trinidad, Guyana, St, Kitts and Grenada for the newspaper.

Three things from those missions still resonate with me.

The first being that I concluded very early after my arrival in St. Kitts that Kittitians were even more polarized than we were in Jamaica. For the animosity between those in the hierarchy of the Peoples Action Movement (PAM) and the St. Kitts Labour Party seemed to run really deep.

Of course this animosity never manifested itself in a violent manner as it does in Jamaica, but it was certainly so intense that when you were in the presence of those from the opposing parties, you could feel the hatred. I suspect they have long resiled from that attitude as one now hears nothing but good reports from those who now observe their elections.

The second was the experience I had in Trinidad. The election I had observed was the one where the Peoples National Movement (PNM) which had for years had a stranglehold on the country, was democratically removed from office by the National Alliance For Reconstruction (NAR) under the leadership of the Late A.N.R. Robinson. That was in 1983.

I will never forget my sheer horror as I attended the last public meeting of the PNM which was held at Savannah.

It was a huge, enthusiastic crowd with all cheering loudly for their party. Suddenly the cheering was interrupted by the announcer saying a NAR campaign vehicle was coming through.

Forgetting I was in peaceful Trinidad, I waded through the crowd toward the oncoming vehicle, fearing that a hostile reception was awaiting those in the invading vehicle. I could not believe my eyes, for as it passed slowly through the thick crowd which had blocked the street, those in the vehicle and those in the crowd started shouting pleasantries at each other as some in the crowd rocked the vehicle plastered with NAR posters, in a playful manner.

211

This left me speechless for with our recent experience of extreme electoral violence in Jamaica, I really did not know others in the Caribbean practiced their politics in such a civilized manner, since we all had a similar history of slavery, violence and colonialism!

The least pleasant and most challenging experience I had observing elections during that period was Burnham's last stand as leader of the PNC in Guyana, (the only English-speaking country in South America,) before he died in 1985.

At that time Guyana under Burnham's leadership was going down the same road as Jamaica had under Manley in the 70's. As a result, there were chronic shortages all around so the government was very unpopular. They however managed to "win" that election using massive fraud and intimidation.

The only difference was that whereas in Jamaica, guns featured prominently, thank heavens those weapons had not invaded Guyana to any degree, so the violence there was not as lethal.

As Burnham had no doubt long planned to use foul means to take those elections, he clearly did not want any observers, not even from a CARICOM country. So, from the Gleaner applied for my visa to visit the country and observe the elections, problems emerged.

I was being sent there a week before the actual event so I could observe the process and not just the voting, but when I got the visa, I was given only a three day stay in the country.

I remember the frustrations I experienced as I was sent from ministry to ministry in that country to try and get an extension of the visa. In fact, it took me almost the entire three days to get the visa extended to the seven days!

In Jamaica, the Gleaner dominated the media landscape, being the only daily publication lasting for over a century. So, they were able to get away with paying journalists very little.

When a competing newspaper, the Daily News was formed and I was invited to become a columnist at about twice the remuneration, I never hesitated and stayed with that newspaper until it folded.

Then came the Jamaica Record and I again became a columnist with that publication but their outcome was the same.

The only newspaper which has lasted against the Gleaner's dominance is the Jamaica Observer and I also wrote a weekly column for them, writing at first under the nom-de-plume "Schoolie" before a couple years later reverting to writing under my own name.

While continuing to write for various publications including the Amnesty International magazine, the Miami based Caribbean Today and the Money Index, editing several publications for others and launching my own company called *Yard Publications* in 1993, I did enhance my journalism experience by going into radio.

The first stint was with the Jamaica Broadcasting Corporation (JBC) as one of their news analysts, delivering commentary

213

after the major afternoon news at five. It was there that I met Norris McDonald, another analyst who had been a PNP activist. We became good friends and he suggested we develop a television program, drawing on both our experiences in the political field.

We worked on it for a while and even produced a pilot, but the station turned it down.

Quite frankly though, I breathed a sigh of relief when they did, for in preparation for the pilot, I discovered that I would actually not only have to become a "fashionista" but also be prepared to spend a lot of time allowing myself to be "redone" by cosmetologist before each segment was taped and that just was not me!

In the meantime, I had also developed a close friendship with the late Anthony Abrahams (Tony) who was one of Jamaica's most underrated but brilliant minds.

He had been a reporter with the British Broadcasting Corporation (BBC) after leaving Oxford University where he had matriculated as a Rhodes Scholar. He later returned to Jamaica and was appointed our youngest ever Director of Tourism. In 1980 he entered politics and won on the JLP ticket so naturally he was appointed as the Minister of Tourism.

It was under his leadership that Jamaica was again able to regain its prominence as the leading tourist destination in the Caribbean, a position we had lost during Manley's socialist/anti-American period. For during the seventies, the industry had sunk to rock bottom as vitriolic and hate filled anti-American rhetoric was being directed at visitors, most of whom were coming from the USA, which is where in excess of 75% of our visitors have always come.

Like all brilliant people in the Jamaica Labour Party however, it was not long before Abrahams was sidelined by Seaga.

He was also terribly libeled by the Gleaner because of a kick-back racket involving advertising and Public Relations contracts given out by the Jamaica Tourist Board to an American firm, when he was the minister. Abrahams was eventually cleared of all charges as it was proven that he had no knowledge of the kickback scheme or had any part in it. He eventually won the libel case with an award which was the largest in the Caribbean at that time, but his career both locally and internationally, had been almost virtually destroyed during the *fourteen* years the case spent lumbering through our antiquated court system.

Looking back though, had Tony not had an extended period when he was not employed, morning radio would probably not have been revolutionized in Jamaica, evolving from music and trite entertainment to programming filled with informative and valuable discussions on current affairs, both local and international.

I cannot remember the exact date that this began to evolve, but it was sometime in 1996 at a time when the media was being liberalized in Jamaica with several new broadcasting licenses being awarded and parts of the government-owned JBC being divested thus bringing competition to the two dominant stations. (The privately owned RJR and JBC).

The divestment of sections of JBC was driven by the government's huge losses on the entity, thus influencing their decision to privatize.

I remember how excited Tony was when he called me one day to say he had an idea for a new type of radio program in the mornings and wanted me to help him develop it. At first, I did not buy into the format but as he explained it, his enthusiasm overwhelmed me and I too became excited.

For weeks after that we would get together in the mornings, analyze various aspects of the news as it related to the economy, international affairs, and since we both loved politics, we always included discussion on the political implications of every development in our own country.

That is when the realization came that we could not simply do the program with presenters but would need to have a good panel with experts who were excellent debaters, drawn from academia, business, entertainment, the political parties etc. (Hence the "club".)

Once we had perfected the format and decided how the program would flow, we determined that we would need an attractive name and spent some time coming up with several, bouncing them off all who were prepared to listen. It was actually Jackie Chacko, Tony's girlfriend who is now a very successful Attorney at Law in Barbados, who came up with "The Breakfast Club," the rationale being that the program would be aired in the early mornings while persons were at breakfast and we were going to have club members participating. It was the perfect choice so we all grabbed at it.

The next step was to start building a panel of experts who would be prepared to get out of their beds in the early mornings to participate (without payment!) Not only would they have to be knowledgeable in certain areas too but also, they had to be dynamic speakers who would not send people back to bed (with boredom.). While this was initially a difficult sell to some of the persons we considered, we found enough people who we figured we could start with.

After weeks of slogging from early morning listening and viewing newscasts both local and international, reading all newspapers and news magazines we could get our hands on, (these were not available on-line then) analyzing the news, bringing in discussants via telephone, commenting and timing our presentations, we felt we had had covered all the areas so we recorded a pilot for presentation to the local radio stations.

This pilot included Tony and I as the presenters and Dr. Trevor Munroe (yup, the same one who had founded the communist Worker's Party of Jamaica in the seventies, which Tony and I had fought so hard against!) and the late Dr. Cliff Lashley, as the "Breakfast Club guests." Munroe and Lashley were both lecturers from the University of the West Indies. (Cliff was murdered a few months later.)

A new concept that Tony wanted to sell to the radio stations was that of revenue sharing. In other words, instead of the station paying us to do the program, he wanted a share of the advertising revenue.

Tony being the marketing man, then sent the pilot to quite a few radio stations but the only one that showed any interest

217

was KLAS FM which was a regional station with its operations in the small mid-island town of Mandeville. They were however in the process of setting set up operations in Kingston and were on the lookout for programs with nationwide appeal.

Klas had emerged on the newly liberalized media scene early, as the government owned JBC radio which had operated regional substations, Radio West, Radio North and Radio Central, was being divested.

Radio West, headquartered in the city of Montego Bay in the western parish of St. James was sold to private investors who renamed it Hot 102. Radio North which operated from the town of Ocho Rios in the northern parish of St. Ann was sold and renamed Irie FM. Radio Central headquartered in the mid-island town of Mandeville in the central parish of Manchester, was sold to another set of investors who renamed it Klas FM and they kept their headquarters in Mandeville.

It was an extremely distressed Abrahams who called me a few days later to say Klas FM loved the program but he could not go with them as there was a major difficulty. They said they would only go with it if Beverley Manley, who was on their staff, worked as the co-presenter with him as "he and I were both two well-known as anti-Seaga people!"

I was not only horrified at the thought but livid.

To begin with, while we both had problems with Seaga's leadership style; had been vocal about it; had left the JLP as a result; how could we be considered more anti-Seaga than someone coming from the bowels of the PNP when the parties

218

were sworn enemies of each other? We therefore concluded that this was just an excuse being used by Klas FM in an effort to find a useful function for Mrs. Manley who they already had on staff.

I did not know Beverley Manley personally but knew of her as a former broadcaster at the JBC who had later married Michael Manley. She had not however been a behind the scenes wife but rather an influential personality in the regime of the 70's as head of the Women's Movement of their party. And we still blamed that party for not only bringing our economy to its knees but also for threatening to bring to an end to our freedoms, including press freedom, to which we had become accustomed and held dear.

Further, Mrs. Manley had not been especially loved by women, except the supporters of her party, as during the period when we had chronic shortages of basic products including sanitary napkins, she had been most cavalier in suggesting to women that we revert to the use of *old cloth* as a substitute, which had been the practice during the days of slavery.

I therefore rejected the very thought of her benefitting from my long hours of working with Abrahams to develop the program and told him absolutely no way, so we would have to find another media house.

However, as time elapsed, it became clear that no other media house was prepared to take a chance on a new concept for morning radio and I realized how terribly disappointed he was that the program could not be aired as he would never do anything without my consent.

I also concluded that I was being selfish by not agreeing to stand aside. For the program had been Tony's idea and although he had put most of the effort in developing it, he would never go with Klas FM unless I agreed.

I therefore called to tell him to feel free to run with Klas FM. He balked for a while but eventually went in with them. He had wanted me to stay on as the producer, but I told him there was no way I was going to work with Beverley Manley.

Time proved that my efforts had not been a total loss however as my daughter Michele did join them as a producer when she graduated with her first degree from the UWI. That was her first job and she received invaluable training as her teacher was Tony himself.

Anyway, before she went there, I was still upset for quite some time and even refused to listen to the program despite Abrahams" frequent pleas that I listen and give him feedback.

However, the program quickly started to gain great popularity among all my friends who were current affairs buffs. Amusingly, they not knowing of my input in its creation kept telling me to listen to this new and exciting program on Klas Fm!

I cannot recall how long I resisted before finally starting to listen and I was instantly impressed at how well Beverly Manley meshed with Tony as a presenter. For one of the original concerns between us had been the fact that we live in an extremely politically polarized country and he had severe reservations about how he would relate to someone who had come from the bowels of the PNP, considering the experiences of the 70's.

They however became excellent working partners and it was not long before I had to admit to myself that the management of Klas FM had indeed made a wise decision. For on the national scene, this program was helping to break down political barriers and hostilities as people saw that there could be civility between political opponents at the highest level.

It was not only at the level of presenters that the political diversity existed though but also among the club members who were gradually drawn from every stratum and represented every political stripe.

It is said that imitation is the best form of flattery, and it was not long before that program format started to have such a positive impact on listeners, that several other radio stations, including those who had rejected the concept initially, started to use the Breakfast Club as a template to develop their own morning programming.

So successful was the program that Tony eventually used it to purchase a radio station, FM 93 and immediately called to tell me he wanted me to be a presenter of a proposed evening edition, called "The Supper Club."

By that time however, I had gotten involved in the real estate industry and become excited to discover that this was the perfect occupation for me because not only did I earn good commissions but more importantly, it allowed me to structure my time around my own schedule. I had therefore totally lost interest in sitting in a studio for hours on end on a regular basis and indeed that was mainly why I had even turned down offers from two other radio stations to have my own call-in program.

For I had also become the alternative host of Jamaica's most popular radio call-in program, Straight Talk which was moderated by the late, great "King of Jamaican Talk Radio", Wilmot (Motty) Perkins. Having built up such a great working relationship with Motty who was also my close friend, I was not about to go to another station anyway, unless he moved his program, for although it had often led to my downfall, loyalty had always remained my strongest guiding principle.

I had met the Perkins'' shortly after returning to Jamaica in the early 70's when he was a columnist at the Gleaner and his wife Elaine was Jamaica's foremost radio dramatist.

We had become close friends and when they first travelled to Malvern in my home parish of St. Elizabeth with me to visit my ailing mom, Elaine immediately fell in love with the area. She did not stop until she found a lovely old house there, totally restored it and subsequently moved to live in Malvern full time.

By then, Motty had left the Gleaner newspaper to go into radio. First, he moderated Public Eye on JBC radio and then joined Hot Line on RJR. When he moved to the county, he became the first moderator of "Straight Talk" the call-in program which was being broadcast from the studios of Klas

FM in nearby Mandeville and which laid the basis for its huge success in radio to the point where they could even move their head office to Kingston and keep the Mandeville operation as an out station.

Shortly after the Breakfast Club fiasco, I was surprised to get a call one day from a Tomlin Ellis, the then General Manager of Klas FM.

According to him, the station needed to identify someone who could sit in for Perkins when he had to be off. Further, as Motty would shortly be going off for three days, Ellis said he was taking the opportunity to audition three persons during the period to see who would be the best fit, whenever necessary.

Not knowing of their plans for expansion, I of course told him I could not travel all the way to Mandeville to do the program and that's when he assured me they had established studios in Kingston, so it was not a problem.

On the given date, I went to their Kingston studio to conduct the program and was surprised when Tomlin called me a week later to say if I was willing to take up the job, they were ready to fly with me as substitute host of "Straight Talk".

I was of course greatly honored to have been selected to conduct the program when the great man was away.

Since the real estate industry is one where the motto is "half a commission is better than no bread" I had no difficulty finding colleagues to handle my business at the shortest notice whenever the station required my services, so everything

223

worked out fine for the decades that I was Perkins" alternative host, wherever he went.

For during the many years of our association, Motty took his skills to other stations and eventually he accepted that he had to make his name and special brand a business so went ahead to copyright and register it as "Perkins on Line".

The first station to benefit from the immense popularity of "Perkins on Line," Motty's interviewing skills and superior knowledge, was Hot 102.

Finally, he settled in at Power 106 and I moved from station to station with him every time, until his death on February 10th 2012.

That date is one that I will *never* forget.

For quite a few years, I had been in the habit of traveling abroad to spend the Christmas holidays with family. This is because my entire immediate family lives overseas. Christmas 2011 was no different in that regard.

When I returned in early January 2012, I had barely landed before I was told that Motty had been missing from the airwaves for many days; there were various other moderators carrying on the program; and the rumor was that he was gravely ill. I immediately called his home and it was a very distraught Elaine who answered the phone. She told me I should come to their house immediately.

By then they had moved back to the capital city and had been living in Stony Hill, a suburb in the hills of St. Andrew about

6 miles north of Kingston. I immediately rushed there but was not at all prepared for what I saw.

For upstairs lay my mentor and friend, barely conscious. Then the real shock came for Elaine confided that his cancer that had been successfully treated six years before and been in remission had returned and the doctor had given him just *three weeks to live.*

You could have hit me down with a straw as I tried to process the information, for the concept of a dead Motty had never ever entered my head. It took me quite some time to recover from that revelation.

As they owned the program and she did not want the uncertainty to continue, Elaine insisted that I return immediately to moderate it for him until she knew what the future held. I did not know how I could ever manage to do the program knowing that at any time I would get the news that my mentor had died, and I would most likely have to make the announcement. But I had to.

I called the general manager at Power 106, Newton James and told him I was back and would resume moderating the program and he was clearly relieved as the distress of knowing that Motty was ill and having to move around staff to try and keep the program going, was having a toll on everyone.

While it is only the listeners who can say how I coped in the ensuing weeks, although I tried to act as normal as usual, inside me, my head and stomach were in total turmoil.

Turmoil because Motty was dying and turmoil because I feared that I would get the news of his passing while on air and would go totally to pieces. Further, although the family wanted to keep the severity of the illness from the public, listeners seemed to have sensed the doom and gloom that I had been feeling. So, people kept calling in desperation to find out how their dear friend and "teacher" was doing and if the rumors of his imminent death were true.

Although I didn't want to do it, I had to keep stifling my conscience by replying, "hopefully he will soon recover and return to the airwaves shortly," for I had promised not to divulge anything about his illness. All this while I was fearfully aware that he could not return as each day his rapid deterioration became more evident.

As the third week approached, I just could not take the internal pressure and tension any more for I feared I would hear of his death any minute, so I told the general manager I could not continue.

He understood the strain and I took my leave, waiting nervously each day to hear that the doctor's prediction of *three weeks* had come true. It was with a feeling of relief that I saw the third week come and go with him remaining alive, although he never got any better. For he was in and out of the hospital during this waiting period but I still kept holding on to the vain hope that the doctor was very wrong and he would miraculously recover.

Feeling more confident as the days passed and the news of his passing never came and knowing that Elaine was depending on me, after a few days, I eventually mustered up the courage to call the general manager to tell him I would return to the program on Friday February 10th.

Fate can be terrible though for would you believe that at 2 am on Friday 10, 2012, just a few hours before my return to the program, (the program aired from 10 am-

2.30 pm) a distressed Elaine called to say Motty was dead.

Up to now I cannot say how I conducted the program that day, only breaking down once.

I did ask Newton James for a copy but even now, some four years later, I have never had the courage or nerve to listen back to it.

Motty Perkins was the longest serving talk show host on Jamaican radio and I dare say no one will ever equal him in terms of knowledge, delivery, popularity *or even being hated!*

He was extremely exceptional too, in that during his long career as a journalist, as politicians and other power brokers tried to silence him and even bankrupt him, he was sued for libel 28 times. But not one person has ever been able to win a libel case against him although his detractors even included judges and a sitting prime minister. (Michael Manley.) So knowledgeable was he about the libel laws.

Motty always preached excellence and he practiced what he preached. So while many of us may think that preparing for a program such as his just meant simply keeping current and being glib, watching my hero work, always reminded me that excellence does not come by chance but only through a level of dedicated hard work that few are prepared to undertake.

For apart from what everyone else does to keep current, every day Motty would have about five tape recorders going from 5-10 pm, recording *every* newscast and current affairs program on the credible stations. Then he listened to and analyzed everyone every night before going to bed.

Henry Wadsworth Longfellow was indeed correct when he wrote;

> *Lives of great men all remind us we can make our*
> *lives sublime, and, departing, leave behind us,*
> *footprints on the sands of time.*

After Motty died, I remained with Power 106 moderating the Friday call-in slot only. It was called "Joan Williams on Line."

That suited me perfectly for I have a permanent interest in social/political affairs, so it gave me a great opportunity to spout off on all the issues I would like to see addressed without having to do extensive preparation, as it was only aired one day per week!

That I continued doing until the end of June 2016 when I had to start preparing for my departure from Jamaica to finalize a two year project in the USA

My ultimate ambition however remains to become a travel writer as both travelling and writing remain my passions.

Sure I travel as much as I can afford to now and blog about every place I go, but serious travel writing would require me dedicating my time to meet deadlines for travel magazines and I just haven't reached that point in life yet.

MY CUBAN CONNECTION

The only reason I visited Cuba in the early 80's after taking part in that bitter *anti-communist* campaign which ended in October 1980, was because a favorite aunt of mine, Aunt Bell who lived in Canada, had told me how absolutely beautiful the island was. As I respected her views to the max and we both love travelling to new places, I decided that since Cuba is literally next door, it was time I visited.

I had been there before with my parents when I was quite young and the country had not yet become communist but I really did not remember much about it.

When I told some friends about the plan to visit to our closest neighbor, they all thought I was crazy since I had been such a high profile anti-Cuban activist who was still writing anti-communist articles the in the Jamaica Record newspaper at that time. Some even swore that I would surely be locked up and quite likely be shipped off to Siberia!

Anyway, despite having some reservations about my safety, I was so drawn by the picture this aunt had painted about the natural beauty of the island, that I decided to take my two teenage children on a one week vacation the following summer, even insisting I was going although we could not get a confirmed flight to return one week later. Of course, I never forced my kids to go but they trusted my instincts on travel so were always prepared to hop a plane with me wherever I was going.

Not being totally mad however and certainly no fool, I expected that the Cubans, having been so active in Jamaica, would most likely have had a complete dossier on me which might cause me to be harassed in their country.

So, I got in touch with the local Cuban-aligned communist party, The Workers Party of Jamaica (WPJ) and told a friend of mine there of my plans. I then asked for a contact in that island who I could call on in case of emergency.

She thought it quite funny that someone as vocally anticommunist as I would want to visit the island but obliged me with the name and phone number of an individual there who was employed by the Jamaican government to assist Jamaican students who were studying there.

For although the government had changed and we no longer had a pro-Cuban regime in power, the scholarship program that Fidel Castro had given the Manley government in the 70's, to try and influence the public that Cuban interests in Jamaica were strictly altruistic, had remained intact.

So off we went, only to discover when we arrived that all my tourism assumptions about Cuba were totally misguided. For I had not even bothered to make a hotel reservation, figuring that the hotels there were empty anyway. Then I discovered to my despair that nothing could be further from the truth.

You see, while the Americans were boycotting Cuba, I soon discovered that their tourism industry was still booming with visitors from Spain and other European countries, as well as Canada, South America and even North Korea, all flocking to the scenic island in droves.

When we arrived at the airport and made enquiries about getting a hotel, we were directed to take a cab to Hotel Central in Havana which controlled all the reservations for the city and nearby provinces. It was when we had done this that we discovered to our horror that all the hotels in the city were indeed booked *solid.*

That's when the serious pickle my laxity had landed us in, dawned on me.

Sure if I had been travelling alone it would have been easier but with two tired, vulnerable and miserable teenagers, I recognized how my uninformed attitude towards our neighboring island had been not only dangerous but stupid.

At that point, with nowhere to stay, I even envisioned us being taken to jail as the Cubans would not be tolerating foreigners as "street people" and worse, persons with no confirmed flight out of their country!

I did not realize that our serious dilemma had been observed by an onlooker until we were approached by a young Afro-American who said she had been living in Cuba for years and had married a Cuban. She immediately told me she had overheard my conversation, seen my distress and offered to help.

However, it immediately it occurred to me that this was all too coincidental so she must be a member of the Cuban secret service or some political cell, but with no other options, I eagerly accepted her offer.

Accompanied by her ever smiling husband, she immediately went up to the central booking desk, had a brief conversation with the clerk there and in no time returned to tell us all was well as she was able to get us a large room at a nearby hotel.

She then explained that the hotels were fully booked as it was summer and during that period, Cubans were allowed to visit and stay in the hotels for two weeks, all part of the greatness of the socialist system, I thought cynically but silently.

While I found the information, she volunteered counter to everything I had heard about that country, I was not about to ask questions, but nodded and expressed our extreme gratitude to her for finding us somewhere to stay.

For the rest of our vacation, both she and her husband proved invaluable to us, telling us where to visit and the fun things to do while calling often to see how we were doing. Despite them being very nice however, I just could not dismiss the queasy feeling in my stomach that they were assigned to us, probably to make sure I was not up to anything subversive, for they kept popping up "accidentally" nearby whenever we visited tourist spots.

However, as everything they did or suggested enhanced our stay, the nervous feeling in my stomach eventually declined.

Would you believe too that they invited us to their small apartment for dinner on the night before we left! That was so wonderful for it was clear that they did not have much but were not only willing to share with us but also even offered a parting gift, some dried coconuts. I had to point out to them that it would be like taking coals to Newcastle so I could not accept them. But I was and still am overwhelmed by their simple generosity, even though I still felt they had been assigned to watch me.

I had to admit though, that it was not only that couple who were very nice and helpful, for almost everyone we interacted with was so polite, charming and helpful. Everyone told you hello on the street and they all assisted in every way possible when asked.

For example, while I am comfortable with Spanish, the Cubans tend to speak extremely rapidly and have their own dialect, so I was having some difficulty understanding a lot of what was being said. However, I remember clearly how on the second day there, as I passed their television station near our hotel, I went to the front desk to get directions to the airline office. The lady there could not assist but she never stopped calling around until she located someone who spoke English and could give us directions.

On another occasion while taking a bus I asked a lady sitting beside us for directions, only to have her disembark at the appropriate stop, walk us to our destination and vehemently refuse to take any money, even enough to repay her bus fare for the rest of her journey.

Having been exposed to the Cubans in Miami, many of whom had totally turned me off by their rudeness and arrogance to the point where I even tried to avoid using the Miami International Airport for connecting flights, and had stopped going downtown Miami to shop, I was really totally bowled over by the open friendliness of the Cubans living in Cuba.

The uncertainty of our return flight kept weighing heavily on me though and was interfering with my ability to really relax and enjoy the country as I decided we just could not stray far from Havana for we needed to keep in constant touch with the airline in the hope that things changed. This we often had to do in person, as the land line phone service at the hotel went down regularly as did the power supply.

It turned out that not having a confirmed flight to return a week later was proving to be my real challenge, for although I had heard up front that all return flights the following week had been booked solid, I had figured that the situation would have changed before it was time for us to return. For to tell the truth, I had no idea the traffic between Jamaica and Cuba was heavy, having figured that since an anticommunist government was now in place in Jamaica, and the Cuban ambassador/DGI head Ulysses Estrada had been expelled almost immediately after Seaga was elected prime minister after the 1980 elections, the heavy traffic the Cubana airline representatives were telling me about was a myth.

This opinion also proved to be totally uninformed too, for each time I checked, I kept hearing "the flight is full but you can check tomorrow".

Naturally therefore, panic soon set in for we just had to get back home as the kids had summer camp and I just could not afford to be away longer than planned.

Worried and almost desperate, I therefore decided to get in touch with the contact I had been given by my friend at the communist-WPJ party headquarters. I was very pleasantly surprised and in fact, totally bowled over, when my link came to the hotel in person and assured me to not to worry as he could get us out without a problem.

Despite this assurance however, I remained somewhat skeptical. Even so, my kids and I started to do a lot of sight-seeing around Havana, going to the nearby beaches and visiting the nearby provinces. We were really having an absolutely wonderful time, enhanced by the magnificent beauty, exciting history of the country and the simple graciousness of the people.

However, my doubts about being able to return home lingered and even now, I still cannot believe *how* we did.

As I said earlier, the flights going to Jamaica were booked solid but I had been assured by Everton, the young man who dealt with the welfare of our students there, that he would get us home so, we had put our fate into his hands.

On the day we wished to return, he came to our hotel on time to drive us to the airport in his Lada, while constantly assuring us all the way that all was well.

The first surprise came when he did not take us to the regular Cubana airline counter, but instead walked us through a passage towards a small (I think it was about 16-seater) **Aeroflot** jet, telling us that it was going to take us home.

Aeroflot was then the national airline of the Soviet Union and according to Wikipedia, during that period, the largest airline in the world!

Once we had boarded and Everton had departed, I noticed that the plane was brand new, even still having the plastic on the seats. I don't know how many persons were in the cockpit, but there were two flight attendants, huge Amazon-like women, who were as cold as they come and spoke no English.

The real shocker though was that my kids and I were the only passengers!

That is when I started to panic as I was totally convinced that they were going to take us to Russia and I was going to be locked up for life in a gulag for my years of anticommunist activity! However, I did not share my concern with the kids as I did not want to alarm them unnecessarily, in case my suspicions were unfounded.

My worries were indeed misplaced, as the plane flew straight to Kingston without anyone saying a word to us during the approximately one hour flight.

I don't think I have ever been happier in my entire life to see that wonderful city of ours, Kingston.

Even today, I am still overawed that a young Jamaican had so much influence in big, bad Cuba, to the point where he could have gotten the authorities to take three unimportant passengers home safely in a brand new jet *owned* by the great super power, the Soviet Union!

That helped me to finally understand too, how easy it must have been for the PNP to send their gunmen who were wanted by the police in Jamaica, to hide out in Cuba until the heat died down, (as they did with George Flash and Tony Brown.)

For after all getting use of a brand new Soviet Union government-owned jet was a heck of a sign of the vast influence selected Jamaicans had in Cuba.

Yes, Everton is back in Jamaica and has quite an influential job here and every now and then whenever I see or speak to him, I refer to him as "my hero" for I remain eternally grateful to him for getting us home safely and, may I add, in style that summer.

The only reason why I have not revealed his full identity is because I know that there still lingers a lot of resentment in this country against some of those who had close ties to the communist regime during those turbulent years and I certainly would not want he or his lovely family (which I met afterwards) to be victimized in any way.

Neither did my new love affair with Cuba stop there, for I had been so overwhelmed by the natural beauty of our sister isle, that as a regular columnist with the now defunct Jamaica Record newspaper, this anti-communist writer penned a series of articles, praising the beauty of the country and the people.

I did not fail to mention the shortages of basic items in the shops and the long lines I had observed from the hotel window as hundreds of Cubans lined up every morning to receive their quota of milk and eggs, though.

My articles naturally elicited many letters to the editor, condemning me for being bought out by the communists. They only ceased when an announcement came via the press that the well-known Jamaican hotelier (read "wicked capitalist") John Issa, was setting up a hotel at Vadadero beach in that communist isle!

There were more surprises in store for me too, for the new Cuban ambassador was so happy to read the articles describing the beauty of his island, that he telephoned me to tell me that I had not seen anything yet. To ensure that I could see it all and really enjoy his wonderful country, he said, he was inviting me on a one week all-expense paid trip there. He also added that while there, I would have a personal tour guide, a car, and stay at five-star hotels. I was really surprised at this gesture, for really, I had just been writing from my heart about the physical beauty of the island and had no interest in becoming propagandists for the Cubans. I told him diplomatically what my position was but that did not faze him at all.

Several months later, I headed back to our sister isle where, true to the promise, a young, handsome tour guide named Carlos met me at the airport and whisked me off in a brand-new Lada to a fairly new hotel in Havana.

It was really a grand trip with me visiting almost all the major attractions throughout the country. We even visited a huge crocodile farm where I was invited to sample the meat, but luckily I had just eaten so declined. There you could see thousands of the reptiles wandering around within secure borders. That is when I learnt about that huge industry they had, where the meat is eaten, the skin used to make leather goods and the heads to beautify things like handbags and souvenirs.

At that time too, AIDS was a new problem in the region and in Cuba, all sufferers from the disease were separated from their families and sent to a central place for treatment. This had apparently been quite an attractive cottage colony in a resort area, and we even toured the outside areas.

Feeling bold, I told my guide that I would like to meet some Jamaicans and their descendants who lived in Cuba. For during the turn of the twentieth century, many Jamaicans had migrated there in search of economic opportunities, for at that time sugar was king and Cuba was really the economic gem of the Caribbean.

Surprisingly, he agreed and drove me to the province of Guantanamo, the Cuban side, where I met a nice old gentleman around seventy years old. He had never been to Jamaica but coincidentally, his family had hailed from my parish, St. Elizabeth. He spoke English well as he had learnt it in school and listening to Jamaican radio had helped. He also spoke our native language, patois, fluently for he said that is what he had grown up hearing his parents speak at home.

When I was there, our own JBC radio was still in operation and had an extremely strong signal. He told me he listened to that radio station every day. He could tell me lots of things about Jamaica even commenting on the prices of some of our basic foods which he said he found to be very expensive. "How do people survive with such prices," he wanted to know.

Since the topics of incomes, subsidies, prices and the socialist versus the capitalist economy can be long, tedious, complicated and even contentious, I had to let it slide.

He later confided that his one wish was to visit his parents" homeland before he died. He could not remember exactly what district in St. Elizabeth they had hailed from but gave me his surname and asked me to try and find his relatives. When I returned, I did try, but not having enough information, had no luck.

Would you believe though that I also had relatives in Cuba, in the adjoining province of Holguin, but did not know at the time!

I only heard about that side of the family in around 2010 from a relative who lives in Canada. This is my paternal grandfather's side of the family which I confess, even now I know very little about.

What I subsequently learnt from my Canadian-based cousin was that her mother and two sisters had migrated to Cuba at the turn of the twentieth century. Her mom and one sister had moved on to the United States and Canada but one sister had remained in Cuba, got married, had four children so we have quite a large number of relatives there.

I subsequently got an email address for the oldest cousin in Cuba who had learnt a little English from her mom, my grandaunt. It turned out that this grandaunt had also taught English in Cuba but while her only daughter learnt the language, her children and grandchildren speak only Spanish.

After much interaction and anxious to meet these relatives, friends and I journeyed to Holguin province in Easter 2014, my first visit since the guided tour the Cuban government had given me years before.

Holguin was as I had remembered, a pleasant farming province but the city was quite large and developed. What I found interesting on this trip was that Raul Castro, the late Fidel's brother and successor, was opening up the country to business and in the city, on almost every street you could see signs of construction as persons had now bought their homes from the government and were refurbishing.

However, transportation remained a terrible hurdle, for while they managed to keep a number of autos from the 50's going and had quite a few Lada cars, public transportation was terrible.

In fact, in my blog on my return, I wrote in part;

> *On a recent visit to Holguin and Santiago provinces, I found the modes of transportation decrepit and uncivilized. People were packed like cattle into anything on wheels, from wagons drawn by tractors, oxen and horses, bikes with side cars to trucks on which rough covering have been installed, at times allowing you to see only the eyes of the passengers in what would be perhaps, prison lorries in other countries.*
>
> *The roads are also full of very old American cars which run like a charm, a spattering of new Chinese*

manufactured cars and a number of Russian made Ladas. In the cities the novelty is the bicycle taxis which all have umbrellas stashed away to be pulled out when the rain falls.

We took a Lada taxi to the country area where my family lives and the noise from the engine was unbearable.

In that part of the province, unlike in the city where there are single family units and even townhouses, most people live in high-rise apartments which the government still owns. Because those who occupy these units are not being given the opportunity to own their apartments, they were badly in need of maintenance and in fact, in most cases, an eyesore.

According to my older relative, the only time any repairs were done to their unit was in the 70's when they had suffered serious hurricane damage.

In addition to the buildings badly needing a paint job or even an urgent washing down, the floors were raw concrete, indoor plumbing no longer worked and water supply was sporadic.

I actually met more relatives from my father's side of the family on that trip there, than I even know in Jamaica. But their standard of living was really poor, with five adults and three children packed into a two-bedroom flat, and one adult daughter still living with her mom. Although she was married, there was such a housing shortage that she and her husband could not acquire their own place so her husband also lived with his mom!

I soon learnt from my only relative with whom I did not have difficulty communicating, that had it not been for her aunts who had migrated to the (capitalist) west, and their descendant's remittances, their lot would be even worse. For since the break-up of the Soviet Union due to the failure of communism worldwide, overseas subsidies to their country had been cut drastically, so millions of people had lost their jobs, most prices were no longer fixed and the economic situation had deteriorated for everyone.

In other words, the late Fidel Castro, (he died November 2016 at age 90) had with his communist experiment, managed to distribute *poverty* thoroughly, most effectively and equally throughout the entire fair isle!

The real shocker for me however was visiting Santiago de Cuba, for that city which I had visited years before, been so beautiful and pleasant, but in 2014 looked more like Haiti than Cuba.

In fact, on my return I wrote another blog entitled "Poor Santiago" in which I said in part:

> *Most of poor Santiago is now one big, derelict, depressing mess. This is because it has yet to recover from the extensive damage done by Hurricane Sandy in 2012.*
>
> *According to the Cuban hurricane organization; "Reports from the area after the passage of Sandy spoke of widespread damage, particularly to Santiago de Cuba.*

Throughout the province, 132,733 homes were damaged, of which 15,322 were destroyed and 43,426 lost their roof. Electricity and water services had been knocked out, and most of the trees in the city had either been ripped off their roots or had lost all their leaves."

While I found that the historic, official buildings and monuments are in pristine condition, obviously restored and repainted since the hurricane, the residential areas including most of the 132,000 homes there, seem to have had very little if anything done since the devastation.

I will admit that Santiago is the only place in Cuba I have seen brand new homes in Cuba on that trip though. These were constructed just across the road opposite to the 26 de Julio Museum and I had at first thought they were offices or some other type of official buildings until I saw the lady who works in the bathroom at the museum entering one and she told me she lived there.

Anyway, the historic districts are a must visit when you go to Cuba as there is so much to see and learn.

On the other hand, after four visits to Cuba, the historic city center is the only place I have ever seen beggars and persons pestering you to buy everything from tours to services.

The province of Santiago de Cuba itself is really beautiful though with lush, expansive, agricultural

*land on which thousands of acres are cultivated with
healthy sugar cane adjacent to huge ranches where
horses and cattle seem to roam without a care in the
world, while the looming, variegated and historically
important Sierra Maestra Mountains hover
protectively on the periphery.*

*Despite how depressing some of the city now looks
however, I am indeed happy that we undertook the
over 170 km ride from Holguin in our smooth running
1953 Chev (driven by Rashell) to once again visit that
historic province which remains the home of so many
Jamaican descendants.*

While I remained in Cuba to get to know my relatives, I
observed as much as I could, but made sure not to talk about
politics, the economy or freedoms with my family, for I did
not want to get them in trouble for it was clear that personal
repression is still very much practiced there.

The greatest dissatisfaction that my eldest cousin expressed
however, was the constant complaint that she did not have a
passport and would probably die without being able to visit
the nearby home of her ancestors. (Jamaica is only 90 miles
from Cuba.)

And as I roamed about in their small town and talked to the
friendly people I met, seeing for the first time, the everyday
effects of communism on the ordinary people, it really broke
my heart.

I am therefore now even more convinced that the struggle we put up in 70's to keep the Cubans out of our affairs in Jamaica, was more than worth *every sacrifice*.

Yes, while things are economically quite bad here for many Jamaicans, at least „the equal distribution of poverty" is not a feature so there are still opportunities for personal advancement.

For in my book, there is nothing worse than not being able to make any progress in life, regardless of the personal efforts and sacrifices you are prepared to expend.

Now that the wicked dictator Fidel Castro is dead; (he still exerted a lot of influence over his brother and successor, Raul although he had supposedly retired) the terrible animosity with the USA has been reduced somewhat and some sanctions eased through the efforts of President Barak Obama, I hope Trump will continue along that path. For that will allow the long suffering Cuban people to not only throw off the shackles of communism economically, thus improving the standard of living for those who are willing to put out the effort, but also personal freedoms will be restored.

For God knows, those people have suffered enough as a result of the alien ideology which was foisted on them and which has kept them in bondage for so many years.

DEALING WITH DEATH

I suppose it is because my immediate family is so small why I never really had too much experience with dealing with the loss of close relatives.

I remember clearly the first funeral I attended. It was at the Anglican Church in Santa Cruz, St. Elizabeth, and I was about nine years old. I had attended it with my parents but cannot at all recall who died. I don't think it was a relative though but what I remember is how traumatic it had been for me, seeing the coffin go down into the ground and men throwing dirt into the grave to cover it up.

That really blew my mind.

That process was of course used in the days before concrete vaults were used but I do not think it would have made any difference to me. For what horrified me was seeing the coffin going down into the ground and for many years, I had nightmares about being trapped underground.

I suppose that was when I decided that I would never be buried but had to be cremated. I never went to another funeral until I was around twenty years old, when a friend of mine was killed in a traffic accident while returning from a party she had sneaked out to attend. I don't remember that event too well but do recall that is when I broke my boycott of funerals.

I did not know my mother's family very well as my maternal grandfather, who had been an Irish immigrant, died in Panama where he had gone to work in the Canal Zone, long before I was born.

I had met her mom who everyone called, *Granny,* only once. Her name was Martha Solomon and she was a midwife. I still remember her although I don't think I was more than six years old when I heard she died. My memory of her was that she was an extremely tiny, white lady, who I had been told, was a Jewess who had converted to Christianity.

I do remember the occasion when I visited her home though, for how could I forget the experience?

She lived in Chapelton, a small town in the mid-island parish of Clarendon, where they had lots of cane plantations. Granny was also a cane farmer who cultivated the product in some hilly sections of her small property, which were far from the home. Therefore, a donkey was used to transport the reaped cane out of the fields.

I recall clearly how on that visit, on seeing the donkey, my first request was to get a ride and someone complied. I still remember the fall as the creature took violent exception to my presence on his back and took off like a light towards the cane field. I still remember everyone saying how lucky I was that I was thrown off immediately for had I remained on the animal's back, the long sharp cane blades would have torn up my flesh.

I did not consider myself lucky though, since that fall really hurt and I just relived the pain, when I am started writing about it! Needless to say, I have never been on an ass since then, as being thrown off a speeding one is not my idea of being lucky.

Granny died soon after that I believe, and I don't think I was taken to her funeral.

My paternal grandfather was Joseph Marshall but he was, called *Teacher* as he had been a school principal. But I hear he just stayed at home for years, as he had become blind when he was in his 40's and had contracted glaucoma.

I don't remember him much either as he too died when I was quite young. What I do recall is that I had been deathly afraid of him as he had a big gray beard and wore sun glasses to disguise his blindness, I guess. I had never seen anyone with a beard before or even with sun shades so it was to me quite scary and I never went close to him and I don't remember going to his funeral either. (I learnt many years later that he was from quite a large family and those relatives whom I found in Cuba in 2014, were the descendants of one of his siblings).

The closest person to me who died after that was my father Joubert Marshall, also called *Collector,* as he was the head of the tax department in St. Elizabeth.

He died in 1967, a week before I got married. He was only 67 years old and I was quite young. (I refuse to allow you to calculate my age!)

He had been my role model, my hero, my defender.... *my everything.*

He was tall and big bodied and I can still remember how, when I was a child, he would carry me all over our yard on his large, broad shoulders with me resting my chin on his bald head.

He was a great provider, and now living in the city where there are often water restrictions, I reminisce how although we never had public water supply in the country, I never once turned on the pipes at home and found them dry. That is because my father ensured that we had adequate concrete water tanks to take care of our domestic needs and the animals on our small farm as well.

As kids we would enjoy the manual chore of pumping the water from the main tank up into elevated drums from which the water was gravity-fed to the bathrooms. My father even "invented" a hot water heater after it was discovered that I hated cold water and most times when they heard the water running, I was still only dry cleaning! So, he got a huge 40 gallon drum, elevated it on some concrete blocks just above the main bathroom and kept a small kerosene stove lit under it always, so we had hot water on demand.

We had no electricity either but I don't really recall thinking this was a problem, for we did have a refrigerator also run on kerosene. In fact, I really do not recall ever wanting for anything as a child although we had nothing close to what kids take for granted these days.

My father taught me everything he knew about the universe and outer space. He believed passionately in life on other planets so he shared all his theories with me. He was also a lover of Greek and Roman mythology and I would listen in absolute fascination as he spoke about their various gods.

251

That is not to say that he was Polytheist, for he was an ardent Christian. It was just that he was a fan of ancient history and philosophy and when he looked into the vast universe, he believed that there had to be life elsewhere.

Being a devout Christian, he never missed a Sunday service at the Bethlehem Moravian church in Malvern, although I learnt many years after he died that he had been really a member of the Anglican Church.

In retrospect, it was not just philosophy and history that held his interest, for he was the one who taught me from as far back as I can remember, that you should never stop learning and getting a good education, as this was the most important thing in life.

I suppose he was into the school tie thing too as his son (Bernard) Bernie and my cousin (Barrington) Barry who lived with us, both attended his alma mater Cornwall College.

He was also a great pianist and I used to sit beside him paying rapt attention as he reveled in Brahms, Mozart, Shubert, Beethoven and the other greats of the classical era. He loved cars too and regularly tinkered with his own at every turn. I remember always being under the car with him or peering into the engine as he worked, changing oil, tuning up the vehicle or fixing a puncture. And since we lived far from a major town, he used an ordinary manual pump to inflate the tire when he was done!

As soon as I could see over the bonnet of the car, he taught me to side-steer and as soon as my feet could reach the pedals, he would leave the car outside so I could learn to reverse it into the garage. When I nearly wrecked the back wall after failing to take my foot off the accelerator quickly enough, he even padded the back wall with old tires to soften future blows.

As soon as I turned 17, the age to be able to qualify for a driver's license, he took me for the test and after that, whenever we were going anywhere, I drove him.

I suppose I could claim that it is because I had a car so readily available why I earned the dubious distinction of being the first girl to be suspended from the prestigious Hampton Girl's School.

For when my dad retired from the Collectorate in Black River, he started working as bursar at the nearby Bethlehem Training College. As he no longer liked to drive himself, I would drop him at work and drive to school.

It was one half term that some of us came up with the brilliant idea that since I had a car, I should pick up our boyfriends at the nearby Munro College, drive them over to the music room at Hampton where there was a record player and records, and have a private party.

No sex in those days, just innocent fun.

We longed to be with our boyfriends as we only saw them socially once per term when the schools combined to have a party. I remember with great fondness how the boys used to sabotage the generators, (this was in the days before electricity reached rural areas) to cause the party to be engulfed in darkness. Before long however, the senior teachers got wind of such practices, so cars were always

253

strategically parked outside the dance hall in order that lights from the vehicles could be turned on quickly, to expose whatever was happening under the cover of darkness, until the mischief with the generators was corrected.

On the day we decided that our boyfriends would be brought over to Hampton to party, as I drove a white VW bug as did the headmaster of Munro, I was bold enough to drive right to the front of the boy's school and pick up the senior guys who we had selected, for I assumed that everyone would have just ignored my vehicle there as being the headmaster's. For luckily when I arrived there, I saw no sign of his car in its usual spot.

In retrospect, I should have known however, that with all the eagle-eyed old ladies around who served in various positions at both Hampton and Munro in those days, I would never have gotten away with it. But I guess I was too naïve and daring that I never bothered to weigh the odds.

So, on that fateful day, after we had set up our party in the Music Room, we had hardly finished the first dance before a house mistress by the name of Miss Brown, suddenly appeared at the door. In fright, the boys jumped through an open window and ran all the way back to their school, but with my car right in front, I was a sitting duck, so a one-week suspension was the penalty imposed.

I cannot recall if any of the girls there were also punished and I had always secretly resented the thought that the boys had gotten away and I had been the only villain, but just last year I ran into a mid-island doctor who reminded me of the incident.

He told me he had been one of the boys whom I had transported and reminded me who his girlfriend was at that time.

I immediately pointed an accusatory finger at him and complained how all the boys had run out on me and I had to take the rap for all of them. That's when he laughingly told me he had been a *prefect* at the time and they had taken away his badge.

Big deal, one badge does not equal one week's suspension!

Anyway, back to the world's greatest dad.

He had been the senior collector of taxes for the parish of St. Elizabeth and his office was in Black River, the capital of the parish. I was told years later by other persons that he had received many offers of promotion to the head office in Kingston but had preferred to bring up his children in the peaceful, healthy countryside.

He only traveled home on Wednesdays and weekends because our home in Malvern was nineteen miles away and roads were unpaved in those days.

Besides his mom lived in Middlequarters which was only about six miles away from Black River and as my grandmother lived alone, he figured she needed his company too.

All my early life I could not wait for him to come home and was forever hanging on to him or in his lap when he was around. But I remember a lot of his time was taken up signing documents for people in the area as he was a Justice of Peace. And whereas others would set the time they were available to assist those who needed the service, no matter when they came, he assisted them. I don't know if he resented the frequent interruptions however, because for some reason he was just not one to express his feelings verbally. In fact, when I got older, I thought he was just too soft, accommodating and compliant, so lots of people took advantage of his good nature and generosity. For example, I clearly recall how my mother often quarreled about how he was not dunning our butcher for his money. For apparently, he had bought a car from my dad but had not made another payment after giving him a small deposit when the deal was first agreed on.

What really made my father my favorite parent was the fact that he never beat us, although that was the popular method of disciplining children for the least infraction in those days. Well let me qualify that, he never beat me!

I recall though, him grabbing the strap and giving my brother Bernie a good wallop one Sunday afternoon when we had been fighting about something and the noise woke him up from his sweet slumber. Yes, I would have gotten a lick too but I was far more fleet footed than my brother and took off like Usain Bolt. I never returned home until much later when it started to get dark and I figured that he had forgotten. I don't know if he really forgot or not but he was so happy to see me when I returned that he simply hugged me and all was well again.

On Saturdays they would put me on a large, slow moving country bus and we would lumber all the way from Malvern to Black River via the south coast of the parish. The trip easily took about four hours although it was only about forty-five minutes when one went by car.

When we got to Black River, my cousin Ken Ramsey who later became a catholic priest, but was at the time working in the Collectorate, would take me to bathe in the wonderful, blue Caribbean sea on which the town was built and the river named, until my father was ready to drive home.

This is why I have such a hard time coming to terms with crocodiles now roaming around freely *in the sea* at Black River, for in the early days they always stayed down river so we knew to avoid bathing there but were free to frolic in the sea from the bridge going south.

I got the rude awakening in 2011 however when with my fellow cyclists, we attempted to ride from Kingston to Negril which is in excess of 140 miles away, at the extreme western section of the island.

We had departed from Kingston in the wee hours of the morning and arrived in Black River around five in the afternoon. Tired and hungry, we had gathered to eat at a restaurant just south of the bridge.

While the food was being prepared, being hot and tired, I jumped into the sea to cool off. As I emerged, I was shocked when a lady walked up to me to tell me it was unsafe to bathe there as crocodiles were in the sea! If that was not shocking enough, within five minutes of me emerging from the water, up swam a huge croc, past the very spot that I had been.

I had never known of crocs swimming into the sea at Black River in the olden days, for we knew them to be fresh water crocs. I hear it is a regular scenario now though so couldn't help wondering why the lady warned me when I came out and not when I was entering the sea?

But back to my dad of whom I only have fond memories.

When he was 67, he got a stroke and became totally paralyzed, unable to speak and his eyes even expressed a lack of awareness or recognition of any of us. Despite this severe condition, I just figured he would have recovered and had absolutely no expectation that he *could have* died for after all, his family had the tradition of living to, between the late eighties to over a hundred years. So since he was only sixty seven, how on earth could he die, was my logic.

I was therefore totally devastated when I got a phone call at Hertz Rent-a-Car (in the olden days before cell phones) at the Kingston airport where I was working, to say he was dead.

Even now, I have no idea how I did it, but I covered the trip to my home in St. Elizabeth in under two hours. This was a distance of over one hundred miles that normally took close to three hours, as we had no toll roads then, the road was very winding and I was driving a VW Bug to boot. It was as if the car was being driven by a demon as I was determined that if I got home quickly enough, I could have brought him back to life.

When I arrived home and saw his dead body covered with a white sheet and being loaded into a hearse, I literally went berserk, even to the point of wanting to kill the doctor who had worked hard to save his life. I did not think so at the time though.

I don't recall how I went through the funeral service which was held one week *to the day*, before I got married. In fact, I can't even recall how I went through my own wedding ceremony the following week! Truth be told, I had wanted to cancel the wedding but my mom insisted that plans had been too far gone for us to do so.

Now I look back in amusement and wonder if, since my marriage was a disaster, did my dad have premonitions that it would be so, hence his departure a week before doom's day?

Although I remember my father with nothing but great fondness, every now and then I wonder why he had been so morose for although he was always loving and gentle to all of us, he rarely smiled and I cannot recall ever hearing him let out a hearty laugh. This was in such contrast to my mom who specialized in wry humor and always laughed heartily at her own jokes, which more often than not, flew right over our heads.

The reason why my dad was so morose still remains a mystery to me and occasionally it bothers me even now. I suppose that is why I recently questioned my older cousin Father Ken Ramsay about my father's first marriage. (We were never told about that marriage by our parents so I only learnt about it as an adult, from a relative). While he revealed that my father had been devastated when he had come home one day only to find that his first wife had left him for another man, I don't know if that traumatic event could have haunted him all his life even after he had an apparent successful marriage and children afterwards.

Since he never discussed such matters with us, I will never know, so the reason will remain interred with his bones.

When he died, although I continued to visit Malvern on a regular basis as my mom still lived there, I never again went into his room; for knowing he was no longer in there was just too painful.

The next close person to me, who died, was my paternal grandmother, *Schoolie*. Her name was Mary Marshall, but because she had been a school principal like her late husband, everyone I knew called her Schoolie, even us kids.

She was a big, strong woman with nostrils that spread from one side of her face to the other. She also had a hell of a humor and one of her favorite jokes was to tell adults not to bring the kids too close to her, for if she inhaled, they would fly up those huge nostrils!

She claimed she was from the Mandingo tribe of Sierra Leone which was known for its fierceness and I remember clearly the story she told us to prove the point, about how she first rode her buggy over the Black River Bridge.

According to her, an official stationed at the bridge had tried to stop her, telling her that *only white folks* could use the bridge. On hearing this, she said she speeded up the horse shouting to the man that if he tried to stop her she would lash him with the same whip that she used to speed up the horses.

She said he quickly retreated; she went on her merry way and was never bothered there again.

The greatest lesson she taught me however was from one of Aesop's fables; the story about the man and the donkey.

At the time she did not tell me the origin, but it has been such a guiding principle for me since I heard it, probably at about age six, that I keep repeating it ad nauseam.

> *Basically, the fable was about a man who loaded up his donkey with products for the market. He soon met some people on the way who chided him for being wicked for having piled so heavy a load on the poor animal, so he quickly removed some and put them on his own head. Further down the road, he ran into other persons who this time upbraided him for carrying so little of the load while the animal was laden down, so he took off the rest of the load and again put it on his own head. Further down the road, he ran into other people who commented that the donkey looked sick, so he should carry him as well as all the load and he did. Having followed every suggestion and instruction he got, he ended up piling the entire load plus the beast of burden on his head. Of course, the next set of persons he met, laughed him to scorn for carrying the donkey and the load, asking if he didn't know that it was the animal that was supposed to be the beast of burden?*

She said, in this case, he was the real ass!

That important lesson she taught me at that tender age with that story, was that if you remain unthinking and take all criticism seriously or follow every bit of advice you receive, you will make *an ass* of yourself.

Of course, she counseled that we all have a conscience and it should always be my guide and it has. That still remains the most valuable lesson I have ever learnt in my entire life.

Schoolie had been born in 1865; just a few years after slavery had been abolished in Jamaica and she told me a lot about that terrible period, including experiences that her own mother had endured. This of course made me very angry. Seeing my reaction to the tales of brutality and the trials and tribulations our ancestors suffered, she counseled me to learn from the past but not harp on it as we could never change what had already occurred.

It is only the present and future which we have control over, she emphasized, and that important philosophy has been reinforced by my yoga teachers and has served me well all my life too.

Schoolie was extremely wise and her counsel had lessons which have taught me how to deal with almost every possible problem throughout my life.

So grateful was I to her that when I was invited to write a weekly column for the Daily News in Jamaica, I wrote under her moniker "Schoolie" for years, before eventually reverting to my own name.

Apart from the wisdom she imparted to me on every occasion, I loved visiting her home as the surrounding land was well fruited. Her property had nesberries, guineps, tamarinds and all the fruits that kids love to eat, and whenever we went to visit her, we headed immediately for those trees.

I think it was the practice in those days, for as long as I knew her, she stowed her coffin, made of cedar, under her bed. This became a favorite hiding spot for us kids when we played hide and seek as we never at that time saw anything morbid about it.

The only problem I had with her was that, while when I visited her she would give me a few shillings, (before we converted to dollars we used the British sterling currency) I distinctly recall hearing my parents say that she endorsed her pension check *every* single month and sent it all on to Billy Graham, an American evangelist.

That used to really rile me as I resented him getting everything every month (all four pounds) while the most I ever got was five shillings! So, it was not surprising that when she and I had one falling out, it was over him.

This was when I was a teenager and she came to live with us. Her room was beside mine and she used to turn the radio up very loudly to listen to him preach every single morning. I now vividly remember the morning; I was having what I thought was a nightmare. During the dream I found myself in hell walking on hot coals and being chased by a monster with a fork which was red hot.

Then I woke up to find that it had not been dream but in fact it had been Billy Graham preaching loudly on the radio, about such a scenario which sinners would have to deal with.

Annoyed that she had played her radio loudly and put me through the trauma of "living in hell," I quarreled with her. She immediately sent a man who worked with us to get a car to take her home as she was not going to live in a house with a rude teenager, she told my horrified mother.

That was the only conflict between us that I can recall, but we made up quickly after that.

When I moved to Kingston and eventually got married, I did not visit her as often as I should, but kept in touch by mail.

Her death did not at all come as a surprise to me as she died in 1976 when she was 102 years old and had been bed-ridden though mentally alert, for almost a year.

I missed her though and especially her wise council. She was buried in the family plot which lies beside the Moravian Church at Middlequarters, in St. Elizabeth, which was built on the land she donated, and where she had been the organist for as long as she was able.

My mom died in 2002, at age 90. She had suffered from Alzheimer's for five long years and that had taken such a toll on all of us that her death was met with more relief than sadness.

She had been a stalwart in our family and the real disciplinarian, for as I said above, my dad only came home on Wednesdays and weekends.

While he was away, we never had a car to take us around for she never learnt to drive until he retired from the Collectorate and even now we often say laughingly that she never really learnt to drive! For she believed in living on the clutch of the car (as there were no automatic transmission cars on the roads at that time) and whenever anyone saw her thundering down the road in my father's huge American Ford car, they would get out of the way rather quickly. I suspect that I ended up as my dad's full time chauffeur because he was deathly afraid of driving with her, as we all were.

She was a very generous person though and no neighbor could ever go hungry if she knew about it. I recall too that every Sunday afternoon we had to take dinner for the shut-ins who lived close by.

She also fostered a number of children, starting with my cousin (Beverley) Betty who was orphaned early and lived at our home from before I was born. She became my big sister. The same with Barry my other brother, who was really my father's nephew but who also, lived with us from before I was born.

When I left home, she escalated the "adoption" process and I never visited home without meeting at least one more new "brother."

She was a very capable farmer too, livestock that is. Her specialties were cows and chickens although we did have a few pigs and rabbits for domestic consumption.

I vividly remember seeing her not only performing artificial insemination on the cows after donning her long gloves, but also helping the mothers to deliver their calves safely. She sold milk and I guess that's why I do not drink the stuff now for we were forever being forced to consume so much as a child. She even made butter for home consumption, with it.

As there was not much to do around Malvern except going to church, I did not at all mind occupying my spare time picking up eggs, helping to wipe them clean, sorting them into the three sizes, then storing them for delivery on weekends to the depot in Munro. I guess I got my great love of farming from her for from I was a child, becoming a vet and living on a farm was my real life's ambition.

However, the vet part got a blow from very early, when I killed my pet baby duck.

At the time, the most widely used medicine for the common cold in Jamaica, was a mixture of white rum and honey. One day, my little pet duck seemed to me to be coming down with a bout of the common cold, so I gave it a teaspoon full of the standard medication and it was with horror that as I watched, its eyes closed and it became stiff immediately. I was so traumatized that I swiftly buried the poor little creature before anyone could know I had committed a gross act of medical malpractice. Even now I sometimes wonder if I had buried the poor creature alive, for maybe it had just been *drunk*!

This is the first time I am confessing to the act and revealing the real reason why I had suddenly changed my choice of profession, for all I had ever talked about when I was a young child, was becoming a vet.

My love of farming remained however, until a man broke into the farm we had in Spanish Town and was killed on my bed. That dream died on that night and from then I have never been able to live in the country again or in any remote place that I cannot see the lights from neighbor's homes. And I don't know of any farms available for the purchase in the city.

My mom was also an excellent and creative designer and seamstress who threw in crocheting and knitting as well, so she made most of our clothes including my very fancy wedding dress and up to when she was quite old, she was still teaching young people those skills in the afternoons at the local community center.

What we kids enjoyed most was her love of baking and experimenting with new pastries. So almost every day there was the aroma of baked goods in our house and on weekends, home- made ice cream was added to the mix.

My parents never drank alcohol but my mother also made an excellent pimento liqueur which she kept for visitors but which we secretly raided from time to time.

For years after I left the country, she remained in Malvern living independently with her new "adoptees" and gave her entire life to every form of church, community and social activity. Like my father too, she was also a Justice of Peace so had regular visits from people who had all sorts of documents to be notarized.

Her social activism did not go un-noticed either for on Independence Day 1983; she received the Prime Minister's "Medal of Appreciation" for Community Service.

When it became apparent that her memory and functions were going and she could no longer manage without medical and personal assistance, she came to live with me in Kingston.

As the Alzheimer progressed however, I did not know how to cope with the strange and debilitating disease, so we put her into a nursing home close by. For the last five years of her life I don't think she ever recognized me or had any idea that she had even borne children.

Although she had all her life been an avid church activist and a generous member, I have never forgotten how the Moravian Church ignored her from the minute she was unable to sign checks to give them to boost their coffers. In fact, it was only when her youngest sister who was visiting from Canada called and blasted them for not even coming to give her communion that they started to send someone from one of their Kingston churches to visit her and do the *bread and wine* ritual.

That is what fertilized my personal dislike for churches and organized religion in general.
She was buried beside her late husband in the church yard at the Bethlehem Moravian Church in Malvern.

That was the sum total of the funerals I attended, until I literally had to face hell itself.

TO HELL AND BACK.

I will never forget *Wednesday 19th July 1995* as long as I live for that was when my entire world came crashing down and that date marked the beginning of my long period in hell.

My only son Thor Nigel Williams was 24 years old and the most gregarious person I had ever known.

His passion had been to become a successful dance hall artist, but despite his popular video and recording of "Nuh gimmi mi nuh drugs" getting good rotation on both radio and television, he never quite made it. (Even now, I hear that song being played on the radio occasionally.) His other big success was Zigzawya which reached the number one position on the British Black Charts.

However, music just did not pay off for him so he got a job as an Entertainment Coordinator at the popular Couples Hotel in Tower Isle, St. Mary. He loved the job, as it allowed him to be on stage entertaining tourists while he honed his craft.

When his girlfriend Michelle got pregnant, he had to face the reality that what he was making on the hotel circuit could not support a family, so he moved to the United States.

He had only returned a few days before Michelle delivered their son Shadrach and was due to fly back out on the 20th July 1995, but he was murdered the night before when he had gone to tell some friends he was leaving.

I had at the time a well-developed routine of putting on my radio headset, my walking clothes and going out to exercise at

7 pm every weekday night. As I laced up my sneakers on the 19th July, the telephone rang and a lady asked for Thor's girlfriend Michelle, who along with my new grandson Shadrach lived with me. I told the caller she was not at home. Suddenly the voice changed moving up to a half shout but quavering badly. Then the person got the chilling words out; "Thor dead."

I don't know how long it took me to process that news but it seemed like it was for hours that my entire body froze. I know it was not hours but I really have no idea how much time passed before I shouted at her to tell me where he was and what happened. I waited for what seemed forever for her reply. In the meantime, I had stopped breathing, my entire internal organs became squashed and a lump developed in my throat which I just could not swallow away and only my brain seemed to be operating. I almost missed the barely audible voice on the other side of the line saying my son had been shot at Markland Avenue and was dead.

The lady was sobbing softly and her words came out haltingly. I don't recall much else but as I did not know where Markland Avenue was, she gave me directions and hung up. To date, I have no idea who that person was, only that she said she was a friend of Thor's.

It was as if I was in a trance and in total mental turmoil as I drove up Upper Waterloo Road and turned on to Shortwood Road as I had been directed, but when I got to Allerdyce Inn, I did not know where to turn so stopped at the gate and asked for directions.

I guess I must have been screaming or something as the guard immediately told me he had heard a gunshot and pointed out that it was Markland Avenue across the road. I estimate that this area was less than two miles from my home.

I drove to a nearby gate where I saw a small crowd gathering, parked and walked to where the crowd was. On the ground at the entrance of the driveway lay my dead son, his pockets turned out.

I took one look at him then and never ever looked at his body again as I just could not bring myself to accepting him as being dead.

I then walked down the driveway to the house and asked some people there what had happened but of course everyone claimed they knew nothing.

That is the Jamaican way.

As if a trance I returned to my car, not even looking at the body on the ground as I passed and drove home.

As I reached my gate, I immediately realized that news of Thor's death had already been communicated to those there as I was met by a loud wailing. Up to that moment I had not myself shed a tear for all I had seen and heard was so unreal, like part of a nightmare, not reality.

I don't know how the news spread so quickly as in no time, my house of was full of people expressing their grief.

In Jamaica there is a proverb "good friend better than pocket money" and I suppose that was when the wisdom of that adage really hit home. The only problem was that it was only when my friends started to commiserate that it hit home, for I recall that is when I broke down.

At that time, everything they said sounded like just a distant buzz as I sunk into my own world of grief, all alone. The only thing I remember about that night was that when a friend named Gloria walked in, I said to myself, if she survived *so will I*. For Gloria had previously lost two sons, one who had downed in the Wag Water River at Castleton Gardens, in the north eastern parish of St. Mary, when he was only nineteen years old. The older son had been attacked on their farm by a worker and killed a few years after.

Jamaica is a killing field you know. In fact, just recently a young Jamaican who would never contemplate returning to our island to live, pointed out to me that she at age 40, knew some ten persons who had been murdered whereas foreign contemporaries her age with whom she interacted, either knew no one who had been killed or did not know more than one victim. I suppose that is when it really hit me how depraved our country had become. I only mentioned that remark, as almost 20 years after Thor's murder, it still remains painful to go over those events, but maybe, just maybe, with so many women losing their children in our killing fields, sharing my experiences with readers may prevent them from feeling alone and it may even help *me* to really heal.

As each time I see our murder statistics and am once again reminded just how many Jamaican mothers have had to face the hell I have, I no longer feel that I was singled out by God for this terrible punishment and maybe they won"t either.

Yes, I suppose misery really loves company.

Back to the 19th July 1995.

I still don't know how I got through that night despite all my friends and acquaintances being around and vainly trying to comfort me. Even then, I still thought it just could not be true that my only son was dead. I can't recall even remembering the presence of my six week old grandson Shadrach during that first night.

Thank God for friends though and especially my Guyanese friend Anne-Marie Hines who lived close by. I later learnt that she took over Shadrach's welfare that night and many nights after, as in the early days she would head straight to my house as soon as she came from work, even passing her own home where she had three children, to come and check on Shadrach first. That is something for which I will be eternally grateful, because the shock of Thor's murder had been so devastating for his mom that she had to be tranquilized.

This caused her milk to be considered contaminated so Shadrach was immediately and inadvertently weaned on the 19th July when he was only six weeks old.

It was uncanny, for although he was only six weeks old, after the death of his father, he became virtually inconsolable. It was as if he knew even at that tender age, that a great tragedy

273

had occurred and try as we might, none of us could calm him. Only Anne-Marie could and she did so until his mom could cope again.

Another friend to whom I am eternally grateful too is my *then* companion Donald, for although he did not know how to console me, he never left my side for months to come. I don't think I could have gone through a single day without him.

The worst part was the sleepless nights though, especially when I teetered on the verge of suicide. There was also the inability to eat for weeks on end as not only had my sense of taste gone, but it was as if no stomach existed at all. That is when I went through every event of my life trying to understand why such a terrible thing had happened to me, for I did think I was a good person and terrible tragedies should never happen to good people!

Thank God I have finally perfected the art of removing most painful experiences from my subconscious, for as I try to record some of the grief and torment of those first few months and the immediate years after, I now draw a blank, although I still feel the lump in my throat rising.

To add insult to the injury of losing an only son, the behavior of the police was clearly designed to wreak the maximum pain as the very next day, there appeared in a story coming from the Constabulary Communication Network (CCN), with the allegation that my son Thor had been shot by a householder who he had attempted to rob!

I could not believe that such a story could have been planted in the press but recalled immediately that a few weeks before, the Commissioner of Police Trevor Macmillan, had been carried in a the noon Radio Jamaica newscast, declaring at a service club where he had been guest speaker, that *"Joan Williams is an enemy of the police."*

Payback time, I thought angrily.

His resentment of me had clearly arisen because of an interview I had conducted with him on radio and dismissed his "cleared up" figures as being ridiculous.

Jamaica has since the early 90's been among the top murder capitals of the world and our police had been notorious for their poor record in solving murders. To try and make themselves look good though, the police have used a *cleared* up rate which bears no relevance to reality. For "cleared up" does not mean the number of murders being solved though evidence, prosecution and conviction. What it means is that whenever a so-called "criminal" is killed, the police would put out a statement saying that the victim had been responsible for a series of murders, so numerous crimes were immediately *cleared up!*

Immediately therefore, any number of previously unsolved murders would become instantly solved without any policing being done or evidence provided. I suppose it is because our murder rate is so uncomfortably high why the general public had been happy to accept that story-line from the police for decades.

That was what I had challenged Macmillan about a few weeks earlier while sitting in for Wilmot Perkins on his popular call-in program "Perkins on Line" and that is what had inspired the "enemy of the police" comment.

At the time the comment was made, I had simply shrugged it off as the ranting of a petty-minded person. Besides, I had long become accustomed to the vindictiveness of the police with whom I had a poor relationship because of their constant abuse of human rights, especially against the poor and defenseless.

Though, on reflection, for some time before Thor's murder I should have sensed trouble ahead, but didn't.

For a few weeks before, my mechanic had called me and asked "Which police you did you give a lift to?" As I did not know anyone in the force personally and had no friends who were police, I had laughingly told him "none." He then told me how he had found an M16 bullet, like what the police used, under my car seat.

I had only just left my vehicle with him for servicing, so I immediately realized that some policeman must have planted it there to set me up, for this would have been easy since I never locked my car in those days or even rolled up the windows.

I had immediately called the office of the Commissioner of Police to tell them to put it over their radio system that I had found the bullet so they should not bother to stop me in a "random" search and arrest me for having an illegal bullet. I had even sent a follow-up letter reiterating the point but soon forgot about the matter as I was not stopped by the police for months.

276

It was only after my son was murdered and a news release was quickly put out to malign him, that I realized the full extent of the hatred on their side.

The animosity of the police at the Constant Spring Police Station which was in charge of the area in which he was murdered, was also very overt as each time I called to find if there were any developments in the investigation, I was met with raw hostility. And the vicious attempt by the police to smear our family's name with that spurious press release just added to the pain of losing my only son.

Based on the police's news release too, it was therefore not surprising when the Gleaner newspaper had a headline the next day declaring "Son of Journalist slain in robbery attempt."

Naturally I complained about the slander and pointed to the fact that my son's pockets had been turned out and his jewelry missing when I got there, but only the Jamaica Observer bothered to carry a small report, to the effect that it appeared that he was robbed and killed and not himself been a robber as the other newspaper had reported!

So devastated and inconsolable was I at the events that I was unable to assist in any way in making arrangements for the autopsy and his funeral.

I had been divorced at the time but I must say that had it not been for his father and his family who made all the arrangements and did the leg work, I don't know what would have been happened.

Thor was cremated and up to today his ashes are in an urn on

Thor and Michele

my mantelpiece and they will never be removed.

It is definitely true that while we naturally grieve for the older ones who die, because we never expect to predecease our children, it is the *cruelest blow* of all. So even now, every time I hear of anyone losing a child it is like another wound to my heart, as I can never forget the devastating feelings caused by the loss of *my* child.

Losing my only son was not the only bad karma waiting for me that year, as in October 1995, before I could even figure out how to bring back some degree of normalcy to my life, the news came that my only daughter Michele was in the University of the West Indies (UWI) hospital in Kingston.

She been pursuing her first degree at the University of the West Indies and had been in a car accident on her way home. I can't even recall how I received the news or even how I went to the hospital but it was an overwhelming relief for me when I heard that she was still alive and had only suffered a dislocated leg.

Only a dislocated leg I dare say now, as the possibilities then had been so unthinkable, for in retrospect, had she also died, I would not be around today to even reflect on my past. For I would surely not have been able to bear the double barrel loss of my both children and would definitely have taken my own life.

278

I really don't know how I got through the next few years, for while friends and relatives remain around to bring comfort for a while, once the funeral is over they tend to move on and one must then deal with the loss, privately and alone.
And some "friends" were even insensitive enough to advise that I "get over it and move on," for they really have no idea of the private turmoil that follows such a tragedy.

Whereas it may be relatively easy to recover from the loss of an older relative and even a mate, losing a child is so unnatural that the recovery period is terribly long and painful. Even now, I remind myself that had Thor not left a baby son who needed us, I would most likely have committed suicide, for the urge to self-destruct became almost unmanageable.

Or maybe I would have chosen the easier way out by going stark staring mad, I often reminisce.

But I had no option for such luxury at the time.

Many psychologists have agreed that;

> the grief that follows the loss of a loved one, permeates everything, making it hard to eat, sleep, or muster much interest in the life going on around you. This emotional maelstrom can affect behavior and judgment. It's common, for example, to feel agitated or exhausted, to sob unexpectedly, or to withdraw from the world. Some people find themselves struggling with feelings of sorrow, numbness, anger, guilt, despair, irritability, relief, or anxiety.

279

All the above applied to me as I tried hard to deal with ever confusing and conflicting emotions, the most outstanding being; hating God and even attempting to become an alcoholic. Nothing worked in the short term.

The only thing that kept my feet on the ground and allowed me to retain some semblance of sanity was the presence of my grandson Shadrach, who would now have to grow up without ever knowing his father.

Although his mom and I tried our best to fill the gap, it did cause him some trauma on Father's Day for the first few years when he attended St. Peter and Paul Prep School. For there, he was at the time, the only child in his class without a father.

I cannot forget though the role his granduncle Chully and his wife Erica played in his early years. They had four young children and the youngest, Monique, was only three months older than Shadrach, so she became his closest friend and playmate, Ruth and Carol, his big sisters while big brother Jonathan became his hero and protector.

That wonderful family embraced him totally and he virtually became one of their own, as he spent a great deal of his early life living between both our homes. He therefore never lacked having others his own age around him and the positive example of a solid family with a loving father figure was invaluable. While that helped however, naturally it could never compensate totally as he never knew the love of a father.

As for me, it was only having him and his mom around and watching him grow up, totally oblivious of the grief we were quietly still bearing, that caused the pain to start easing gradually. Knowing how much he would need strength and stability at home, also forced me to remember the disciplines I had been exposed to at Ananda Marga yoga classes where meditation had taught me how to harness inner strength and depend on the God within to overcome all ills. For as Emerson agreed; *"Nothing can bring you peace but yourself."*

Another important philosophy of this ancient yoga Eastern practice dictates that one not concentrate nor hold on to the past but only learn the lessons it offers then concentrate on the present and the future. For while we have some degree of control over or present and future, there is nothing we can do about the past.

I don't think my grandmother Schoolie had been a student of such Eastern philosophies for she was an ardent Christian, but that is a lesson she had also tried to teach me at an early age.

Something else happened to help me heal a little, and to this day I cannot determine if it was a dream or an experience with the *after-life,* so I am still slightly embarrassed to reveal it.

After Thor's death, I was in total mental agony, not only because of the mundane grief we were encountering in this life but also because of concerns about his welfare in the afterlife. For after all, while different religions have advanced theories over the ages, no one knows for sure.

Therefore, motherly concerns caused troubling questions to keep popping up in my mind such as, where had he gone? Was he happy? Was he in torment? Those questions were unanswerable so they would continue to torment me for life, I had assumed resignedly each time they arose.

After going through perhaps months of that type of mental torture, it was as if Thor appeared at my room door one day as I lay in bed. He looked exactly as he always did in life. In fact, I still remember his favorite jeans which frayed at the seams and those were what he had on at that moment.

Startled by his presence since I had been very painfully aware by then that he was indeed dead, I asked him what he was doing here? To which he replied; "I came to check how you are doing mommy." Still in shock I asked him how he was doing to which he replied; "All is well, I have a few tasks to complete but they are no problem." I still remember that conversation as it were yesterday!

Seeing him standing there looking and speaking so normally, I immediately convinced myself that his death had been a terrible nightmare and I was now awake so all was well. I rushed towards him with open arms to give him a hug but my arms seemed to go right through him. I still don't know if this was a dream or not, but a peace settled over me like a cool blanket of mist.

It was uncanny then and still is!

I suppose that is what finally helped me to gradually get rid of the grief and to start thanking God for having given me Thor for almost 25 years and for the great gift of a wonderful grandson and his loving mother who had become part of my small, closely knit family.

Remembering always to be thankful has helped a great deal although I must admit that in my weaker moments when I longed to indulge in the luxury of self-pity, I had frequent bouts of just breaking down and sobbing for no apparent reason.

Thank heavens these bouts became less frequent as time passed.

That is why I can now agree with what the late American author Rose Kennedy wrote; *"It has been said that time heals all wounds. I don't agree. The wounds remain. Time -the mind, protecting its sanity - covers them with some scar tissue and the pain lessens, **but it is never gone.** "* (My emphasis).

So true, for now, even over two decades later, the grief of losing my only son remains poignant and distressing to accept.

Being able to look back with less emotion now however raises a particularly puzzling change in my attitude.

I had always been a strong advocate of capital punishment. Somehow though, after my son was killed, I never cared whether his killer was caught and was to be hung. For as far as I was concerned, the only thing that could comfort me and bring closure was me waking up and finding that it had all a terrible nightmare and that he was not really dead. So after a very short while, I really stopped wondering who killed him and why, as nothing could bring him back.

I suppose I was forced to take that practical approach since our police have an abysmal crime solving record.

For even now in 2016, less than 5% of the "murderers" are being convicted. And the majority of what the police manage to effectively garner the evidence for is domestic, where the killer is more than obvious.

So even if the police had not been hostile to me from day one, they most likely would never have solved Thor's murder anyway, so why think about having the murderer killed or even the existence of capital punishment, I have long surmised.

What has now started to bother me since 2014 though, a serious suspicion that maybe Thor was actually assassinated by someone in our own police force!

For decades, the Jamaican police have been notorious both locally and internationally for their habit of carrying out *extra-judicial* murders under the guise that they had been attacked by criminals.

Finding guns to plant on these victims was never a problem either, as revealed in the infamous "Kraal massacre" which was widely publicized both locally and internationally. During the trial that followed that massacre, the shocking revelation was made in court that the police had gotten the gun they planted on the victims from a political don aligned to the government in power at the time!

That evidence was given by none other but a policeman who was at the scene and who gave evidence for the prosecution. (He has recently been reiterating the charges via podcasts, from a safe haven where he has resided since put into the witness protection program.) Incidentally, the police prosecuted in that Kraal *show trial* which the government was forced into having by human rights advocates, were found not guilty. For as usual it was the police who investigated police murders and they had their methods of deliberately contaminating and manipulating the evidence as well as intimidating witnesses.

However, that particular massacre by the police was so troubling that the US embassy seemed to have been particularly attentive. For when the Wikileaks cables were released, a number of them dealt with the Kraal massacre and the ensuing trial. Although the police involved who were charged were exonerated by our local courts, the US embassy revoked all the visas of the police involved.

Unfortunately, because murder is so frighteningly commonplace in Jamaica and we are anxious to hear there are fewer murderers around, the majority of Jamaican citizens, though insisting they are Christians, have always appeared to approve of extra judicial killings. For why have they so happily swallowed the police" version with regard to these killings no matter how incredible, has always been the question some of us keep asking?

Indeed, for decades, the police had used the same template to report such killings simply changing the *names, dates and places* where the killings occurred. The standard text was always;

> *A man was killed when he confronted the police with a handgun. Reports are that about ....am/pm, a team was on operation in.................*

Upon reaching a section of the community of
…………………………, shots were fired at the team.
The fire was returned during which…………..was hit.
The police say he was found clutching a handgun. He
was quickly taken to the nearest hospital by the police
but was pronounced dead when he arrived.

This standard press release has been used even if the victim was shot in the back and eye-witnesses swore all he had in his hand was a ganja cigarette!

To make themselves out to be heroes who slay wicked villains too, the police often painted their victims as criminals who had murdered several persons so deserved to die. (Thus improving the cleared up" rate at the same time!) This unsatisfactory state of affairs has always been opposed by the loud but tiny "articulate minority" in Jamaica and international organizations such as the United Nations Human Rights Council and Amnesty International.

Although the long serving former Prime Minister P.J. Patterson had publicly admitted that "a corrupt police cannot investigate corruption," in 2000, when he gave in to pressure and established the Bureau for Special Investigations (BSI), it was clearly just to appease the loud dissenters. For guess what? That organization had (the same corrupt) policemen and women as the investigators so it should surprise no one that after some fifteen years of operation, *not one* police was ever been charged for murder as a result of investigations by the BSI.

The alarming number of young people that were being killed

286

by the police under suspicious circumstances did not go unnoticed by some courageous Jamaicans however. It was that small group which got together with prominent leaders in the Roman Catholic Church to form the citizen's rights action group called "Jamaicans for Justice" (JFJ) in 1999.

Although they withstood much criticism and animosity for years from vocal members of the public and the police, some of whom even branded them a "criminal rights group," they remained focused and resolute. Their dogged determination to bring extra-judicial killings to an end, finally earned the respect of most of the members of the public although they have remained scorned and hated by the Jamaica Police Federation.

Their credibility increased however because over the years, they were able to provide solid evidence to debunk the police stories, even getting independent coroners from abroad where necessary.

So fearless and thorough was their campaign that even some persons who support Rambo tactics, had to take note. Their struggle had been long, dangerous and hard, but many young black Jamaican men's lives have been saved because of JFJ's exposure of the murderous corruption in our police force.

Their advocacy against *official murder* was noted internationally too, not only among the organizations mentioned above but also by reporters worldwide, even Al Jazeera.

This is an international television network which gained respect for its coverage of terrorist activities in places like

Afghanistan. In April 2010, they produced a documentary called "Vigilante in Uniform," which dubbed our police force as being among the "deadliest in the world".

The thing is, while in the USA, murders by the police are usually based on inherent racism, in Jamaica where blatant murders by the police are far more prevalent, it is a matter of black police killing black civilians. In fact, so deadly are our police that young men have been killed on quite a few occasions for simple things like smoking a spliff. (A small marijuana cigarette!)

After the JFJ established credibility locally by demonstrating time and time again that young men were being killed for no other reason than being confronted by power crazy trigger happy police, or because of personal animosity, they were finally able to get the support of Bruce Golding who was heading the JLP in 2007 and was hoping to become prime minister.

He promised in his election campaign that his party, if elected, would establish an independent body to investigate questionable police killings.

The JLP won the election and a strategic review of the police force was carried out by the Ministry of Security in 2008. Among its findings were:

> *The dominant culture in the police force was corruption and this reigned even if it meant violating legal and ethical boundaries; some police were contract killers and involved in weapons trafficking; the police were regarded with distrust by the public*

and generally perceived as being corrupt so they
could not get cooperation in their investigations; they
treated the public with disrespect and constantly
violated the human rights of citizens, etc.

Finally, based on those findings, in 2010, an oversight body
called The Independent Commission for Investigations
(INDECOM) was established.

Initially, the police tried everything, even going to the courts
on a regular basis to challenge the powers given to that
oversight body and when they could not defeat them there,
members of the force involved in extrajudicial murders and
some of their colleagues even started to deliberately
contaminate crime scenes before the independent
investigators arrived.

Even today, the Police Federation continues a propaganda
campaign to try to discredit that body while frequent threats to
murder INDECOM investigators are being reported.

Despite these difficulties, the effectiveness of the agency
finally started to be fully felt in 2013. In 2014, they were
eventually able to reach the point where they could arrest
some policemen for murder. This is an excerpt from a press
conference held by INDECOM on Feb. 4th, 2015:

The Independent Commission of Investigations
(INDECOM), the agency that probes abuse
allegations against the island's security forces, has
charged 53 police officers with murder. The police
officers accused of unlawfully taking a life, make up
the large majority of the 84 officers before the courts.

The psychological effect of having an independent agency to investigate questionable police killings has been significant too for by 2014, the number of police killings had seen a huge decline as reported at the same news conference. For there the commission revealed that;

> it recorded 129 fatalities by security forces in 2014, a in 50 per cent drop in fatalities from 2013, when 258 people were slain.

(Can you believe that in a little country with a population under 3 million, the police had been killing upwards of 250 young people annually!)

Can you also believe that just by virtue of police being finally held accountable for extra-judicial murder, there was a drop in those questionable killings by over 50%?

The reason why I have given such a lengthy background on extra judicial killings is because for years, I had been under the impression that this was the full extent of the murderous campaign by members of our own security forces. For if the police could so easily get public acceptance for murdering many innocent young men some of whom were their enemies in domestic relations, why would they need secret squads to murder others surreptitiously, pretending it was being done by "criminals unknown" I had reasoned. Even when the Gleaner newspaper carried a story in January 19, 2014 declaring that an anonymous retired senior cop had confirmed that death squads existed within the police force, I remained skeptical.

It was not until INDECOM started to arrest the members of an alleged police death squad that I became convinced that the extent of police murders did not stop at so-called shootouts. (They have arrested 11 alleged members of one death squad so far in Jamaica while applying for the extradition of one who had fled to Canada. Note these 12 cops are supposedly members of a death squad in just *one* parish. We have 14 parishes!)

Despite having nothing but mistrust for the police for years, I was actually stunned by this revelation by INDECOM, although I had long and often publicly said that nothing that happens in Jamaica shock me anymore.

Interestingly, the Police Federation appeared to support the operations of the death squad, for in a report on August 21st, 2014 in the Jamaica Observer regarding the alleged miscreant held in Canada, they said in part;

> *THE Jamaica Police Federation has sought the intervention of the Government to secure the release of a Jamaican policeman now in custody in Canada. Constable Witney Hutchinson, 28, who is accused of being part of a death squad in the central parish of Clarendon, was arrested by the Canadian authorities in June, following a request by the Independent Commission for Investigations (INDECOM). The Canadian authorities claimed Hutchinson is being held on the basis that he's a threat to public safety.*

The Police Federation claimed the policeman was being unlawfully detained and that INDECOM had no authority to apply for his extradition!

This uncovering of the death squad therefore started to cause some people to wonder just how many of the victims that we had assumed had been "murdered by criminals" were actually killed by those armed by the taxpayers to "serve and protect?"

These are the official murder figures for Jamaica for the past 8 years and it is interesting that a *reduction* in regular murders also *coincided* with the birth of INDECOM.

<u>YEAR PERSONS MURDERED</u>

Year	Number of murders	
2007	1674	
2008	1601	
2009	1680	
2010	1278	
2011	1124	
2012	1097	
2013	1280	
2014	1005	

While a reduction in extra-judicial murders committed by the police would be expected to decrease radically when they finally faced the danger of being found out and prosecuted by an independent oversight investigatory body, why did ordinary murders committed by so-called criminals also start trending down with the lowest number in 8 years being in 2014?

It was this death squad development and the strange decrease in murders coinciding with INDECOM's effectiveness which gave rise to my suspicion that it is quite possible that it was the police who killed my son.

Why?

> *a) He was killed shortly after Commissioner McMillian publicly identified me as "an enemy of the police."*
>
> *b) My house phone was always tapped (and so clumsily done that it did not take anyone using it any time to realize this) so they would have no difficulty knowing the movement of anyone in my household.*
>
> *c) That would explain why they could so quickly produce and dispatch a press release saying he had been a robber for,* **it was on ice.**
>
> *d) There was open and clear hostility towards me by police at the Constant Spring station as evidenced in their attitude each time I called to find out if there had been any developments in his murder investigation.*
>
> *e) Thor was clearly assassinated by a marksman, one bullet to the heart.*

"*e*" above is particularly interesting, for as far as one can gather from the information put out by the police over decades about the outcome of shootouts, the *only* real marksmen in Jamaica are in the police force and the army. For during the decades when they killed an average of over 250 young men per year, claiming the victims were killed in shootouts, less than 008% police involved in these "shootouts" were ever killed or hurt.

On the other hand, the police were *clearly marksmen* and their accuracy even defied the boundaries of possibility many times. For example, when they shot and killed 5 young men in 2001 in the parish of St. Catherine, during the highly publicized event dubbed the "Braeton Massacre," their own reports declared that the men had been firing at them from inside a house. When the shooting was over however, not one policeman was hurt but all five men were dead, *each* with gunshot wounds to the head!

So, if the police are to be believed, not even James Bond could equal our policemen and women when it comes to marksmanship!

I have no way of proving or even being 100% certain if they killed my son and really I don't seriously care either. For nothing will bring him back and that is the only thing that could appease me.

However, this latest suspicion only reinforces the opinion I have always had that those who are sworn to serve and protect us are *extremely dangerous and corrupt,* and the regular reports of policemen being caught committing all types of other crimes from ordinary housebreaking to murder, extortion and fraud on a regular basis, is not helping.

Neither am I alone in this perception, since in a 2014 study done by the Latin American Public Opinion Project, (LAPOP) revealed that more than half (50%) of the Jamaican public showed low trust of our police and a full quarter (25%) said they did not trust our police, period.

Anyway, although life has never been the same after Thor's death, he lives on and is always loved and cherished in all our hearts.

No, I am no longer distraught, depressed and dismayed, and I keep his flag flying high in my best-selling book, **The Original Dancehall Dictionary** which is distributed worldwide through Barnes and Noble and Amazon.

The Dedication reads;

This publication is dedicated to my late son Thor Nigel Williams (13/8/71-19/7/95). Thor was a disciple of dancehall and in fact he cut several records under the name Daddy Tar. Of the lot, one, Zigzawya, did quite well and became number one on the Black British Charts for several weeks. He however enjoyed his job as an Entertainment Coordinator at the Couples, Tower Isle, as that offered him unlimited opportunities to perform on stage with both resident and visiting bands. It was his enthusiasm for dancehall which exposed me to the emerging language (the new street lingo) and inspired my research which led to the birth of the first edition of "Original Dancehall Dictionary" in 1993. At the time of his untimely

death, we were working on the Second Edition and I know he is happy that this publication has become a bestseller and that I have continued to upgrade it. **Thanks Thor**. *Your spirit lives on in many ways and definitely in this publication."*

Yup, as Pastor James Ford reiterated; "you never get over it, you only go through it."

So, life goes on.

RELIGION? COUNT ME OUT!

It was Thor's death more than anything else which led me to start thinking seriously about religion and the afterlife.

I grew up in a conservative Christian family where we went to the Moravian Church for at least three hours on Sundays. My mom had been a Congregationalist and my dad an Anglican, but because this was the closest established church to us, that's where we went.

The only good memories I have about that period of *compulsory* church attendance is that we had homemade ice cream waiting for us on our return from church on Sundays. For we had an ice cream bucket and the ritual was for us kids to turn the bucket manually until the ice cream hardened, then they stuffed the sides with newspapers to keep the cream solid until we returned home.

In addition to the long tedious Sunday rituals, we had bible reading followed by prayers *every* night at home.

As a child, I remember I even spent many sleepless nights trying to figure out how God came about.

Then off to Hampton School I went and this was an Anglican school, where every morning we had to go to chapel. So, it was not unexpected that I was forced to become confirmed as an Anglican when I got to the mature age of 15. That ceremony was performed after many months of preparation and it served a very useful purpose in that when I had to take my Senior Cambridge exam, I knew the bible so well that I did not have to study at all for the Religious Knowledge segment. I got a B in that exam without even trying.

As much as I disliked it therefore, having the bible shoved down my throat in the early years was indeed beneficial in my studies and even now, when people raise issues of religion on my talk-show, I often surprise both my callers and myself, (most members of the public have long written me off as being an atheist) by still being able to recall and recite some stories from the bible and can even quote a few popular verses occasionally.

However, I have always found religion very tedious and irrelevant to my life. So, I never attended church again once I had left home, until my daughter became a teenager and got very involved with the Church of the Rock in Kingston.

Her involvement had me dropping and picking her up from a youth program there called "Rock Teens," on a Friday night. While waiting for her, I found myself being attracted by the vibrancy of the music I heard streaming from their building for they had a very appealing, modern music ministry.

That form of worship I found most enlightening and I remember as a child how drawn I had been to the loud music and chanting coming from a "Pocomania" church within earshot of our home. I loved hearing their pulsating, *rootsie* music, the pulsating beat of their drums and the loud singing, and had always wanted to attend.

Because Pocomania worship was regarded as some form of devil worship or black magic in those days, even mentioning that I would like to visit that church was considered a mortal sin!

So being attracted by the music at Church on the Rock, I started to attend on Sundays, for the music though, not for the message. For it never took me long to realize that they were addicted to the Old Testament and I just could never relate to that *version* of God.

Although I never prayed often or had any great relationship with God, to me She was always the great creator of the universe and *all good.* On the other hand, listening to those who said they were Christians spouting the Old Testament, the God they described was a wicked, vengeful creature who had no qualms about even slaughtering children and extracting vengeance from all humanity for eternity because poor Adam and Eve are said to have sinned.

In other words, while they are always praying to God for forgiveness, they simultaneously promote the philosophy that God herself is *not at all forgiving*, as she is determined to punish all man and womankind *forever*, because of Adam and Eve!

Then there is the Christian endorsement of *incest.* For that is what the acceptance of the Christian version of creation and the story of Noah implies.

And even in this enlightened age, those Old Testament Christians cannot understand that scientifically, this creation theory would cause the human race to be weak and totally defective because of the inbreeding.

Since so many so-called believers like to quote the holy scriptures to justify a myriad of evil things that they do, (Like slaying one's enemies a la David, as a local gunman once told me!) I often wonder how long it will be before some of the old testament touting practitioners of incest who destroy their families by so doing, start citing the bible's creation/Noah stories to justify this terrible and disgusting practice.

Another big turn off for me too is the fact that Jews and many Christians paint God as a *bigot* who created several races but adopted one, the Jews as "His chosen people."

Absolute hogwash.

When I think of the gall of promoting the Great Creator as a bigot, it really solidifies my dislike of Christianity and the Christian god. The rhetoric at the Church on the Rock therefore got to me after a while, so I quickly returned to my life as a non-church attendee.

However, I still felt a need for some religious fellowship so started visiting Swallowfield Chapel. They had a similar music program to Church on the Rock, (but not as vibrant) but again I found their religious doctrine way too limiting, so gave up going to church entirely.

So, while as a child, I could not wait to leave home to free myself from the tediousness of boring, traditional religion, my leaving those churches years later was to free my consciousness from the terrible picture being painted about the "good God" by so-called enlightened preachers.

Even now, as I observe the majority of the upholders of the Christian faith in Jamaica, it never ceases to amaze me how much they fear death, more than any other religious adherent that I have ever encountered. It is as if the faith they proclaim so loudly about "God's protection" is all a lie and the thought of dying and going to heaven, which they tell us is a place of eternal peace and happiness, scares the hell out of them totally!

For as someone who has been a political commentator for so many decades, it always bowls me over how quickly the most ardent Christians use the "I am afraid" excuse when challenged to stand up against ills in the society, or how often they ask me if I am not afraid for my life, because of some opinions that I express freely and openly.

However, I remain a great lover of gospel music. I also love and respect those churches which are dedicated to assisting the poor, so never fail to express my high regard and admiration for the "Salvation Army," (the evangelical part of the Universal Christian Church) and to a lesser degree, the Roman Catholic Church. For organizations such as these, I often publicly contend, would be what Jesus would have founded if he was here on earth today.

Otherwise the Christian philosophy is just not for me, although it is almost impossible to avoid hearing it being espoused non-stop in my country which is reputed to have the largest number of churches per square mile in the world. (But is also among the top 5 murder capitals of the world!)

In fact, had my children not spent some time living with their maternal grandmother, I don't think they would have seen the inside of a church.

The experience of living with my mom and going to church regularly, was not at all totally counterproductive, for my daughter, when she was a teenager, not only became a member of "Rock Teens" and an active member of the Church on the Rock itself but also a member of their choir. So, I consider my mom's influence to have been very positive as opposed to the choice some of her friends made to become party animals.

However, she did at one time become so fanatical that she once even destroyed her great modern music collection because she claimed that the music *was sinful.*

It is also the various types of fanaticism I sometimes observe among many Christians, which scares the daylights out of me!

I will never forget the time I had gone on a classic car run in my sports Volvo. This is the one with the fish tail which was chosen for the British adventure series "The Saint" starring Roger Moore. It was a really great classic car.

I had been a founding member of the club and really enjoyed the out of town rides when a long line of these beautifully restored cars would be driven to some country area for display and a great *"lyme"* with classic owners from other parts of the island. Anyway, because these were classics are usually quite old, at times some things did not work properly on them.

In my case it was the gas gauge that was not working and with these cars being very heavy, they were usually guzzlers.

I cannot recall which country area I was returning from that day, but I had this passenger with me whom I did not know was a Christian fanatic. On our return journey, just as we approached Kingston lo and behold the car sputtered and I knew immediately it had run out of gas. I opened the door to go out and beckon another driver to get help.

Suddenly the passenger got into frenzy and started a tirade telling me to stay in the car as he was going to pray to God to put gas in the tank! He then started to pray loudly.

Stunned, I tried to humor him but after a while I realized he was dead serious and totally brainwashed so I had to just ignore him, go outside and wave down a motorist. Fortunately, the very first motorist who came along stopped, took me to a nearby gas station, brought me back, poured the gas into the tank and stayed until the car started and we were safely off. His shamefaced comment was, "God sent that motorist to help us."

I was and still am really extremely concerned about some of *madness* I hear being imparted to vulnerable people by some of our churches!

After the devastating blow of having my only son Thor murdered, as Christianly just was not my thing, I started to read extensively about other religions, trying to get answers for my own personal tragedy or maybe I was really searching for something to hold on to.

For decades I had been a great admirer of Louis Farrakhan but could certainly never embrace Islam because of its crazy, demeaning attitude towards women. I eventually decided that Buddhism was the religion that made the most sense to me for it espoused such a peaceful, tolerant and non-violent philosophy.

A lot of what they believed too meshed with the practices I had been exposed to while doing yoga many years before and which I had found so comforting. So, one night I attended a Buddhist ceremony which was being held at the nearby Terra Nova hotel. Having been exposed all my life to the vibrancy of Christian gospel music however, it did not take long for me to decide that mere chanting just wasn't my thing.

Besides I was an ardent carnivore and while I always felt sad when I saw animals being fattened for the table, those thoughts fled the minute the meal was prepared.

To comfort myself a little though, I have already decided that no matter where I reincarnate, I will be a vegan in my next life as I just do not have the discipline to make such a sacrifice in this life!

Eventually, I decided that formal religion was just not for me but the best bet was to adopt the best practices from them all and that would become my own *personal* religion. Anyway, these religions were all founded by men and I really do not see where men are more inspired or closer to God than women are, so why not?

My aim for this life therefore became: my own personal development, being at peace and becoming a really good person.

For while being a good person is critical to accumulating sound Karma for the next life, it also plays a huge role in what happens to us in this life as well, as whether we like it or not, we will be punished or rewarded based on the Karma we create.

I know this belief in Karma has made me a far more deliberate and considerate person, weighing the consequences and implications and accepting the biblical advice that one should treat others as how we would like to be treated, before taking any action.

Key to my newly adopted philosophy too, is the acceptance of the *limited role* that God plays in our lives. For She determines when, where and to which parents we are born; and when, where and how we die. These things we have absolutely no control over. For while we have some level of control over most of what happens to us, our birth and death remain totally in the control of the Creator.

It has really been liberating to develop/accept these philosophies, especially the element of having no control to which parents we are born to and in what country. This gives me the impetus, no matter how terribly things are going, to thank God every single day for allowing me to have been born to a wonderful family in this absolutely beautiful island of Jamaica and not somewhere where women are basically non-people or where personal freedoms do not exist or even to a horrible family where children are sold into slavery or ravished and abused.

Since I have also come to accept that our hour of death is preordained, it has brought me peace and made it much easier to come to terms with my son's death.

The acceptance of this theory was not something I jumped at just to make myself feel better, for as I look back at many incidents in my life it certainly makes sense. For example, how come I slept peacefully and emerged unscathed as bullets were fired in the bed beside me when two men fought furiously to get control of a gun? And what about the time when my daughter, then twelve, ran across the road, fell under a speeding car yet emerged without a scratch? This was years ago when I had taken her and her brother on vacation in Europe and she had disembarked from a tour bus and ran across the street in Germany.

As I reflect on life, there have been so many times when I should have died but was not even injured while so many friends and acquaintances have succumbed in weird and unthreatening circumstances called "freak accidents."

No one therefore can ever convince me that our time and place of death is not *predetermined*, so I suppose that is why so many people seem to think I am courageous and fearless, in terms of the some of the commentary I make and the activities I have been involved in.

Actually, living in Jamaica, this philosophy has served me very well, for being in a country that falls in the top five murder capitals of the world, can be very stressful if we really concentrate on our personal safety.

In fact, I really think it is the strain of existing in "dangerous" Jamaica that causes so many of my countrymen and women to develop diseases aggravated by psychological pressure, and drives such a multitude to migrate every year, desperately searching for places where they think they can live in relative safety!

Quite frankly, in my book too, if more Jamaican "Christians" trusted God, stress would really not be such a negative factor in their lives would it?

I have also decided that my best option in life is to build a personal relationship with God who gave us the intelligence to create and succeed in our own endeavors. So, while I can comfortably forget the whole religion thing and often have scintillating debates on local radio with "believers" and religious fanatics who proclaim loudly that if you are not a Christian you are lost, I am certainly not an atheist.

You know, a close relative gave me this amusing explanation as to why he is an atheist. According to him, he had been told so much about praying to God for everything and leaving it all to him, that he did not bother studying for his senior Cambridge exam many decades ago, so naturally he failed it. For the repeat exam, he studied fervently and passed. Since then he has continued doing everything on his own and is today a successful doctor with an extremely happy and accomplished family!

Jamaica is quite a hilarious country to live in though, for although we are among the top five murder capitals of the world, and most of us endorse corruption totally, most people claim to be Christians. Try rejecting Christianity in a place like this therefore and what happens? You are immediately branded an atheist! For dogmatic, narrow minded chauvinists even go so far as to make God out to be such a petty, vindictive, evil being, that she would condemn Buddhists, Muslims, Taoists etc. to eternal damnation for not accepting the great prophet Jesus as his only son and God in the flesh.

With such parochial attitudes all around, I am happy I am not a Christian for Christianity to me has become synonymous with intolerance.

An Adventist friend whose wedding I attended some time ago even ran into me one day and laughingly told me how long he wanted to see me to tell me about something that happened at his reception.

According to him, as he sat at the head table during the reception I walked in and a lady said to him "Isn't that Joan Williams" to which he replied yes. He said within minutes he heard "The atheist is here," buzzing all though the room as people pointed me out. Of course, we had a good laugh as he reported the occurrence to me.

You know as I reflect on the various turns my life has taken in the search for truth and inner peace, I am now convinced that the death of my son Thor has in a weird way, made me a much better person. For before I had to contend with all the turmoil, emotions and sadness that came with his loss, I was really quite careless about life and the implications of our existence and most importantly, Karma.

Now having read widely and analyzed the theories others have developed over the years on the meaning of life, spiritualism and all that, it has caused me to do serious introspection on a myriad of matters, attitudes and values that I have held over the years, all for the better. So today, I find myself far more concerned about the welfare of others than I had been and more importantly, extremely grateful to God each day for life, health, happiness, peace, success, the safety of my family and all the things that matter.

I suspect that the "Christians" who are reading this confession have already fallen on their knees to pray for the eternal damnation of my soul! What are they going to do when they learn how I had once promised God to become an evangelist? This was of course before my eyes were opened to the fact that there were other religious philosophies.

I had been travelling from Colon in Panama to the San Blas islands, a trip by boat which lasted around three days. I have never had a worse trip in my life, for the boat listed dangerously in super turbulent waters, for most of the journey, after about a day into the journey.

That is when I promised God that if I survived, I would become an evangelist. Thank God however that an evangelist is one who preaches the *gospel* and unlike a lot of parsons who mount the altar and proclaim things that they do not believe, I won't do that. So, since I do not accept the teachings of the *gospel* as the unvarnished truth, I certainly cannot now keep that promise!

I am proud to say that today I am one of the happiest persons in the world, partly because I suspect, I have rejected religion totally and like Helen Keller, have come to accept that:

> *Your success and happiness lies in you. Resolve to keep happy, and your joy and you shall form an invincible host against difficulties.*

EXPERIENCES WITH GANJA (MARIJUANA)

On February 24, 2015, the government of Jamaica enacted legislation decriminalizing possession and use of small quantities of ganja, but it has been so widely and openly used here for so many years, that a visitor from Mars would have long thought that smoking pot in Jamaica was as legal as drinking rum.

One of the first things I learnt as a young Jamaican migrating abroad in the olden days, (the late 1960's) was that there was a popular view that we all smoked ganja and even always had some to share!

I had grown up in rural Jamaica and lived there most of my life before migrating to Canada and was not spared this type of reception. Not with hostility but conspiringly, as our ganja was rated by the young people I met there, as the best in the world.

Problem was, I had never seen or smoked ganja up to then, for at the time it was not accepted in the conservative middle-class environment in which I grew up. In fact, it was frowned on as something only used by laborers or mad people with locks, as Rastafarians were regularly described then.

So when I was bombarded with questions about ganja and requests for samples from young friends in my new country, I was totally discombobulated but not as disconcerted as when on the insistence of two of the young neighbors in the apartment building in which we lived, I tried it. For although at the time I had been smoking cigarettes, the initial drag on

311

the butt that they offered me, burnt my lips more than anything I had ever felt before and I was not all impressed by the weed, to the disappointment of my "irie" friends.

My next attempt at smoking ganja was not until some years later when we were touring North and Central America and arrived in Guadalajara, in the western pacific side of Mexico. As we arrived in town, we were hailed by a carload of young teenagers, who on seeing our Canadian license plate, were anxious to welcome us to their country, practice their English and show us a good time.

And show us a good time they did, including introducing us to their "Mexicana gold" which they claimed was the best marijuana in the world. I have no idea if it was, for unlike the taste I had gotten in Canada which only turned me off as it burned my lips, I got a good draw from the spliff they made for me. I don't know how many draws it took me to get totally smashed but I certainly did get very confused and wobbly that day.

Although I was quite young and willing to experiment, I did not like feeling intoxicated and not totally in charge of my thoughts and actions that the experience left me with, so decided then that ganja was just not for me.

When I returned to Jamaica, there was a totally different attitude to ganja than when I left, for now it was hip to smoke it but I still resisted the temptation for quite some time though.

Oh yes, I did try the ganja tea. This was at the urging of one of the workers on our farm, named Douglas. He was a Rasta man and never stopped telling me how healthy it was to drink ganja tea regularly. He planted about a ¼ acre of the herb beside his home on the farm, for personal use and to earn a few extra dollars. So, at his insistence, I tried the tea. It tasted bland and had absolutely no intoxicating effect on me, but since he convinced me that it helped boost the immune system and kept one fit, I started to drink it every morning as I figured it wouldn't kill me.

Then disaster struck for him.

As it happened, police from the Spanish Town station were one day passing though the farm while chasing a miscreant and they saw the plot of herb. As it was not yet ready for reaping, they said and did nothing. But would you believe that a few weeks later when it was ready for reaping, they returned and told poor Douglas that they were eradicating it as it was illegal for him to grow it!

Clearly however they were reaping it for their own enrichment, for hadn't that been the case, why did they wait until it was ready for use?

I recall clearly the devastating effect that this had on poor Douglas for this happened a few weeks before Christmas. He bawled "living eye water", as he had hoped to sell the crop to earn extra money to have a very merry Christmas! I never saw him plant anymore and if he did, it was not where it could be easily detected.

Anyway, he never gave me any, so as the supply ceased so did my use of it as a tea. I really do not know if it was a healthy or harmful drink though as it had absolutely no visible or psychological effect on me.

Some years later after I had returned to live in Kingston, one night when some friends visited me at the townhouse where I lived at the time, they seemed to be feeling so good about life while they were high on the weed, that I decided to join them.

Big mistake.

To begin with, as soon as I had taken about the third draw, a terrible hunger descended on me and although I recall visiting the kitchen several times and snacking on everything I could find, it was as if my stomach had become a vast chasm and whatever I ate was having no effect. I can't recall how much I smoked that night, but what I am not allowed to forget up to this day is asking "Who is Joan" when they got ready to depart and told me goodnight!

I think it was after that night that I pledged (once more) never to smoke ganja again as the embarrassment caused by that question was devastating and lasting.

And it is a pledge I kept for many years before once again yielding to temptation, telling myself that since I was much older, my ability to control myself after a few puffs of the product that was making so many of my friends feel so *irie,* was by then fully developed.

Further I had a close friend who had one of the most brilliant and creative minds I had ever seen in anyone and there was never a time that I saw him that he was not smoking his "spliff."

Maybe I was thinking that it was cause and effect in his case and to tell the truth I wanted to be as brilliant and sharp as he was. So, one day when he offered me a drag off his *sensimilia* (a special type of our ganja) which he had stuffed into a ginseng pipe that he was using, the urge was too much.

That was when I took my final and lasting pledge never to smoke ganja again as long as I live and I know I will never go back on that pledge, ever. For I have never been more confused and totally out of it, in my entire life.

When I left his home, I had to drive about two miles to my own home, but up to now I cannot tell how I got to my place that day. What I do remember though, is that two or three times during the journey, it was as if I suddenly became conscious and realized that I had stopped driving and was just sitting in traffic in the car in the middle of the road!

Totally frightened when it first happened, I thought I would never have made it home, but somehow I did but determined from that day many decades ago, never to use anything that could put me into a condition like that ever again.

Yes, ganja is liberally used all over the world today and I know many brilliant and rational people who use it on a regular basis and have never seen them have an adverse reaction, but one thing I know, it certainly is not for me!

But if you like it, by all means go ahead and have a big spliff (a Bob Marley) and ride high for me.

CONFRONTING RACISM

When I told my daughter Michele who resides in the USA where she is pursuing a Doctorate in Education with the thesis being "The elimination of white supremacy in education," that I was reflecting on some aspects of my life and sharing some events in a book called "Looking Back," she said she hoped I would write about *my* experiences with racism.

I was a bit taken aback at first, since living most of my life in Jamaica; racism is something we rarely consider.

But recalling how even my brother Bernard, who is an OB/GYN and has been practicing at the same hospital in North Carolina for decades, had told me that at times when he is the elevator in his medical garb, white women on seeing him would wait for the next lift, I could appreciate how racism is *ever-present* in the lives of black migrants in the USA.

For it seems to be prevalent everywhere in that country.

I even recall too how when my grandson Shadrach was a teenager, he used to tell me how when he went to school for a short time in "white" Colorado, he was stopped and questioned by police when walking alone on the street, for no other reason than being black. Later, when he first went to university just outside of Tampa, in Florida, he saw *Klansmen* with white sheets over their heads on the side of the road one night.

Besides, with the frightening frequency with which, especially young unarmed black men are being slaughtered by white police and vigilantes, it is difficult for people living in the USA to ignore racism as we often do. Especially since Obama, the first black president in the USA was elected, for some whites have become so incensed about a black man having achieved the highest office there, that the inconvenient harassment that non-whites had previously suffered for simply *Driving While Black*, (DWB) has become far more lethal now, so regularly we are now hearing about young men and women being executed by white police, on a whim.

So, I understood her concern about racism although it is something I had rarely reflected on as I lived in a black majority country. I suspect too, because I had been fortunate in that the only experiences I *personally* have ever had with racism, were non-violent, I had basically dismissed the issue.

On reflection now through, what may shock some people, is the fact that although I have lived in the US, Canada and travelled in "white" countries extensively, my *past* experiences with racism occurred right in Jamaica!

When I told my daughter, she was surprised but encouraged me to reflect anyway.

I now recognize that growing up as a child of a white mother and black father, some experiences that remain entrenched in my memory of early life in St. Elizabeth, were the result of endemic racism which existed in places where remnants of the former British colonial masters resided at the time.

You see, because of the fresh and healthy environment in the cool hills of Malvern where I was born, reputed to be rated among the top 5 best climates in the world, the area attracted a number of the landed gentry. Most of these persons earned their vast fortunes elsewhere however, for Malvern has always been predominantly residential.

Because my father worked in Black River which was some 17 miles away from our house and it took forever to drive to Malvern in those days because the roads were unpaved, he did not come home every day, only on Wednesdays and weekends. My mom therefore had to find ways of breaking the boredom in that deep rural area before televisions were invented.

One item on the social calendar in those days was going to tea with those of her British friends who hung on to that tradition. On quite a few occasions therefore I was dressed up and forced to accompany her. But because I was only a small kid and black to boot, I was probably regarded by those ladies of the gentry as not even being present at all, so they did not have to be too careful when racially based remarks were being made.

For I recall quite vividly how on one occasion, a "lady" commented that "When I walk on the road, I speak and wave to everyone, even a black man. " Incidentally, the speaker on that occasion was the Australian-born mother-in law of Spencer Hendricks, the man who had tried to have me arrested for voting when I was only a child!

Another conversation I recall clearly too came about during a discussion about golf, as we were visiting with a lady who lived right beside the Malvern Golf Club which was then on the way to the prestigious Munro College. She had asked my mom why she did not join the golf club to which my mom replied "But my husband does not play golf." The lady then countered "We were not inviting your husband, just you." I really do not remember my mom's reply to the retort but do not recall us ever going to that home anymore for tea or even seeing her anywhere again!

However, I was not aware at the time that such remarks were *steeped in racism*, for to tell the truth, I never knew that something by that name even existed!

The next experience I had where color was obviously the underlying factor, but probably not a case of racism but rather *ignorance*, happened in Montreal when I was fourteen and had gone there on vacation with my mom and brother.

We were visiting a black family from Montserrat who lived in what was then a white neighborhood but they did not seem to have any racial problems.

However, what I could not figure out was why the white kids, with whom I had become friends, kept insisting that my mom could not possibly be my *real* mom so I had to have been adopted.

For the life of me, I just could not figure why they were having a problem accepting that she was my real mom although it did not have any apparent impact on our relationship. I do recall however that they stopped pressing the issue after my father joined us a few weeks later when he got his vacation.

On reflection, it was only then that they seem to have learnt their first lessons about the vagaries of biology!

Although I was living briefly in New York at the beginning of the civil rights movement and actually worked there for a while, I personally never experienced any racism. I did however have a lot of sympathy for those who had and was in total solidarity with the Black Panthers who wanted to violently overthrow the white establishment instead of using the long, tedious and peaceful route advocated by Martin Luther King Jr.

I was in good company though for both Rosa Parks and Maya Angelou revealed in later years that they too had initially supported the revolutionary path.

Then I moved to Toronto to work and go to school at a time when there were very few Jamaicans or indeed West Indians around, so my best friends were all white. I still cannot recall ever having had to personally confront racism there for although the racial turmoil was escalating in the nearby US, it found no traction in Toronto while I was there.

The last place I had expected to see any sign of racism however was in the San Blas islands which lie between Panama and Colombia. But this was not black/white racism but rather *shade* prejudice.

We had been hanging out with the San Blas Indians who are as dark as I am. And we stayed on the islands for quite a while until we heard from some nuns who had come over from Colombia, that tuberculosis was rife there. We never knew about the prevalence of that or any other disease and had been mingling closely with our hosts. Once we heard about the disease however, we could not wait to leave.

We had ended in the San Blas region, because once we decided to return home from Canada, we had opted for the long way, by first touring North, Central and South America for a couple months.

So off we set from Toronto with our stove, tent, clothes and our basic necessities in a small convertible British made MG car. The plan was to ship the vehicle to Jamaica once we got to Panama then tour South America by public transportation.

It was when we were in Colon, Panama that we heard about the beautiful San Blas islands and were fortunate enough to meet a member of the tribe named John who spoke English, as he worked in the canal-zone.

The inhabitants of those tiny, beautiful islands were extremely friendly and welcoming to us for as we arrived at a new island, John would introduce us to the chief and arrange for us to sleep in hammocks in one of the schoolrooms. One night, as we approached our living quarters, (I think it was the third island we visited) we heard the chief shouting loudly and screaming at two jet black men who had arrived in the early evening and had their hammocks slung in the same schoolroom that we were staying in. They immediately took down their hammocks and moved elsewhere.

We later learnt from John that they were fishermen who had come over from Colombia but the chief was refusing to allow them to sleep in the schoolroom as they were *too black!* This from a chief who was by no means white but rather, colored like us, but he had somehow learnt shade prejudice!

Years later I ran into a situation in Europe which I assumed at the time was based on the racist dictum that "All black people look the same" but realized a few years later that this was clearly not so. I had been flying domestically in Germany but although the practice at that time was only to search travelers at international borders, every domestic airport I landed at, I was body searched. It was only later that I learnt from a friend who spoke German that customs officers were overheard saying they thought I was *Angela Davis*, that I understood a little better, though still remaining a bit surprised.

For those who are unfamiliar with Davis, she was a Californian black activist in the late 60's, who had been dubbed by the racist US government, as a *terrorist*.

During the days of violent national racial unrest, she was the leader of the communist party and also had close relations with the Black Panthers. So, she was quite a force to be reckoned with. She was arrested, charged, tried but acquitted of conspiracy in the 1970's, of the armed take-over of a Marin County courtroom, in which four persons died.

When I had my experience in Germany, Davis had long been rehabilitated in the US and was professor with the History of Consciousness Department at the University of California, Santa Cruz, and a former director of the university's Feminist Studies department. Clearly however, the Germans had not absolved her and still considered her a person of interest or someone to be watched.

322

It was not until much later when I went to Guadeloupe in the Caribbean and the black taxi driver who was taking me from the airport called me "Miss Davis" that I got a shock. I said "No, I am Williams." He however insisted *conspiringly* that he knew that I was really Angela Davis as he used to transport "me" every time "I" visited Guadeloupe.

Poor me, I had never even been to Guadeloupe before!

That is what made me realize that the mistake the Germans made was not necessarily because all black people look the same! Anyway, for the life of me, I cannot imagine how I could be mistaken by anyone for Angela Davis when, seeing her on TV and in newspapers, she appears to be almost white with red hair and freckles and I am very black!

While I was shocked at the prejudice of the chief in the San Blas islands, nothing shocked me more than when I returned to my own country and personally encountered outright racism in the 80's and once from even black people!

The first incident was at a hotel which overlooked the tourism city of Montego Bay, then known as Richmond Hill Hotel. It was reputed to have an excellent restaurant.
I had just flown into Montego Bay from a vacation in Cuba and had run into some friends who told me they were going there for dinner and invited me to come along. When we got there, we sat in the open-air dining room overlooking the city and as we chatted, we noticed that no waiter had come along to take our order although we had probably been there for about 15 minutes.

Shortly after, a group of about four or five white tourists entered and would you believe that before they could even sit down, about three black waiters rushed madly out of a room to see who could get to serve them first! Well we saw red, told them what we thought of their behavior and left. I also wrote a letter to the press about the incident and complained to the Jamaica Tourist Board, but unfortunately did not follow up to see if any sanctions were imposed on that establishment.

The worst incidence of racism that I encountered was at Laughing Waters in northern parish of St. Ann. This is a lovely property with a great house and a waterfall, all of which form part of the area known as Roaring River. The government owns the property but at the time it was leased to a private individual.

Some friends and I had been hanging out in the area and went over to Mamee Bay beach to rent a boat to tour the coast. While we were there, we saw some white foreigners renting a similar boat from another operator there and they pulled out a few minutes before we did.

As we motored along the coast, we saw the beautiful waterfall inland and noticed that the group that had left ahead of us was reveling under it. We asked the boat's pilot about it and he told us it was Laughing Waters and asked if we wanted to stop there. Naturally we did.

We had a wonderful time under that waterfall but were shocked when immediately as the boat with the white foreigners pulled out, a security guard came to tell us it was private property and we had to *leave.*

Right away I discerned what was going down and told him we were going nowhere as this was clearly racism as it was not deemed private property when the white people were there. Poor fellow, he was obviously just trying to hold on to his job for he pointed timidly to an off-white woman on the beach who was looking in our direction and he muttered; "She said you have to leave."

Incensed I walked over to her and told her she was a disgraceful racist. We had a heated argument on the beach with her telling me how she had rented the property from the government operated Urban Development Corporation, (UDC) for thousands of US dollars and *she* would decide who could use the facilities, so we must leave.

I dared her to throw us off and walked away to rejoin the group under the waterfall where we stayed until we were ready to depart.

At that time, I had been a columnist with the daily broadsheet, Jamaica Record but not only did I do a column on that experience but followed up with two others on racism, self-hatred and shade prejudice by black Jamaicans in the island. I had more than enough evidence of that, as it was something I had seen in practice at the JLP headquarters when I was working there to defeat the Manley regime in the 70's. In fact, a group of us youngsters had on one occasion addressed that very issue, when we asked for a meeting with the leader Edward Seaga, to air our grouses on various matters.

Though an uncomfortable topic, racism was brought up to the white party leader because we had observed that when the poor black people who did the grassroots work for the party visited the headquarters, they were often treated with disrespect by the black guard at the gate, but the minute the people of lighter shade appeared, they were immediately ushered into the premises without question. He promised to address it but I never saw a difference.

Back to the racist experience at Laughing Waters.

After our confrontation with the racist, I also wrote a letter of complaint to the UDC which was then under the chairmanship of the late Gloria Knight and it is to her eternal credit, that due to the policies of the lessee, she immediately cancelled their contract.

I was also quite heartened by the response of readers to the articles I had written and felt greatly honored when people like the late Professors, Rex Nettleford and Dr. Aggrey Brown, both internationally recognized social activists from the University of the West Indies, wrote letters to the newspaper congratulating me for tackling that social ill which most people preferred to keep hidden under the carpet.

Shortly after, on running into my ex-husband, he informed me how upset a former friend of ours was with me as I had caused his family to lose the property which was being operated by his daughter! To tell the truth, while I knew him to be a very nice person as was his son, I had no idea the racist was his daughter but would not have done anything differently, even if I had known.

For while I am willing to tolerate many inconveniences and tribulations just to continue living in the wonderful island of Jamaica, racism is just not one.

Amusingly, years later when I set up my real estate dealership, I discovered that the racist lady was also in the business and on two occasions, persons from her firm called me to co-broke properties but I told them I would never co-broke with a firm operated by a racist, no matter how much it cost me.

Postscript

In late 2016, I moved temporarily to Florida, to undertake a two-year project.

My move was made in the midst of the presidential campaign in which, Donald Trump, through his divisive and racist rhetoric, had started to give comfort to *bigots* who were then coming out from the closets in droves.

In fact, around that time, my grandson pleaded to be transferred from the university he attended in Tampa, Florida, as he had become most uncomfortable with the sudden appearance of Confederate Flags on campus there.

I decided to settle in the Ft. Lauderdale area and get a unit in an over 55 complex, where the rates are much better as they get subsidies from the Federal government. However, the government leaves the operation of these complexes to the individual Home Owners Associations (HOAS) which apparently operate as a law unto themselves as they appear not to be answerable to any entity for their actions.

The first one I applied to was located in the "Lime Bay" complex in Tamarac. But would you believe that although I more than qualified for every single criterion they laid out, I was turned down!

I suspect that particular complex was dominated by Jews, for as I waited in the lounge to be interviewed, I noted that the only magazines and newspapers available there were Jewish ones. Further, I was told by a building inspector that most of the complexes in that area were controlled by them.

However, I never had a problem getting into another complex nearby at "Concord Village."

I did not take what appeared to me to be a blatant act of *racism* by the Lime Bay HOA lying down, so immediately fired off a complaint to the Broward County Human Right's Board, but apart from a polite acknowledgement, nothing has happened and I suspect that nothing will, since Trump is now the president of the USA.

And although he was rejected by the majority of Americans (Hilary Clinton won the popular vote by almost three million!) he is the "elected president."

I therefore suspect we will soon be seeing an escalation of more blatant and even violent acts of open racism and anti-immigrant behavior during his term in office.

Sad considering how many people lost their lives from the turn of the century and especially in the 50's and 60's on, to fight for racial tolerance.

The world had even fostered hope that MLK's dream had finally become reality when Barrack Obama was elected president in 2008.

How wrong we all were.

www.ingramcontent.com/pod-product-compliance
Lightning Source LLC
Chambersburg PA
CBHW060835280326
41934CB00007B/795